Religious Experience and Christian Faith

F. W. Dillistone

RELIGIOUS EXPERIENCE
and
CHRISTIAN FAITH

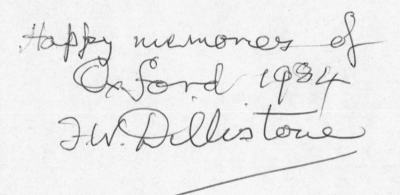

Happy memories of
Oxford 1984
F.W. Dillistone

SCM PRESS LTD

© F. W. Dillistone 1981

All rights reserved. No part of this publication may
be reproduced, stored in a retrieval system, or transmitted, in any form or by any means, electronic,
mechanical, photocopying, recording or otherwise,
without the prior permission of the publisher,
SCM Press Ltd.

334 01422 0

First published 1981 by
SCM Press Ltd
58 Bloomsbury Street London WC1

Typeset by Gloucester Typesetting Services
and printed in Great Britain by
Richard Clay (The Chaucer Press) Ltd
Bungay, Suffolk

CONTENTS

ACKNOWLEDGMENTS

The author and publishers gratefully acknowledge the permission of the following to quote from copyright works:

Faber & Faber Ltd and Harcourt Brace Jovanovich Inc for lines from *T. S. Eliot's Collected Poems 1909–1962*;

Faber & Faber Ltd and Oxford University Press Inc for lines from Edwin Muir's *Collected Poems*, © 1960 by Willa Muir;

Faber & Faber Ltd and Alfred A. Knopf Inc for lines from *The Collected Poems of Wallace Stevens*;

Laurence Pollinger Ltd and the Estate of the late Mrs Frieda Lawrence Ravagli for extracts from *Phoenix* and *Phoenix II* by D. H. Lawrence.

PREFACE

Invitations to write two biographies caused me, during the past few years, to focus my attention on the ninth decade of the nineteenth century. One of my subjects was born in 1885, one in 1884. I became curious to know who were their contemporaries and this led me to a discovery which has intrigued and fascinated me ever since: during that decade, most of the writers whom I have come to regard as pre-eminent in religion and literature were born.

For example: William Temple and Teilhard de Chardin were born in 1881; James Joyce in 1882; Karl Jaspers in 1883; C. H. Dodd and Rudolf Bultmann in 1884, C. E. Raven and D. H. Lawrence and Ezra Pound in 1885; Paul Tillich and Karl Barth in 1886; Julian Huxley and Edwin Muir in 1887; T. S. Eliot in 1888; Arnold Toynbee in 1889. All these attained their maturity in the decade immediately preceding the First World War. They all shared the spirit of that age, even though their physical circumstances and social environments were widely different.

In the process of making myself familiar with Raven's growth and development I found myself asking questions about some of the other figures in this galaxy of famous men. Why, for example, did Dodd and Bultmann, born in the same year, each trained in the best scholarly discipline of his own country, each subsequently gaining international repute in the field of New Testament studies – why did they differ so markedly in their presentation of the central gospel message? Why did Barth and Tillich, again born in the same year, exposed to the same philosophical and theological influences in German universities, ultimately construct such radically different systems of thought as are to be found in the *Church Dogmatics* on the one hand and the *Systematic Theology* on the other?

When an invitation came to deliver the Zabriskie Lectures at the Virginia Theological Seminary, Alexandria, I decided to explore some of these questions in detail by comparing the careers of pairs of writers belonging to the generation immediately preceding my own, whose names have for many years been familiar to me and whose works I have learned greatly to admire. Not unnaturally, my selection of writers has been influenced by my own special interests and by my own sense of indebtedness. Some have for a long time seemed to be companions through their writings and, in three cases, through personal associations. With others my acquaintance is more recent; my knowledge of their works is much less extensive. These studies, then, are in no way the fruit of original research. Their purpose is to compare, and thereby to clarify, a particular issue.

1

The Problem

The generation that attained its maturity in the decade preceding the First World War was exposed to novel and, in many respects, startling ideas. There had been sufficient time for the concept of evolution to become widely known. Theories of relativity and discontinuity began to be debated in scientific circles. Possibilities of psychological analysis and explanation were being actively explored. The confidence of historians was growing as they looked forward to the time when the essential facts relating to human progress would be within their grasp. Students of the world's religions were comparing and evaluating differing faiths rather than resting content with the assumption that Christianity was the unique revelation of divine truth.

Each of these movements of thought was bound ultimately to affect the general religious outlook. If man had evolved through a long and slow process, had religion evolved in the same way? If man's view of the universe was relative to his particular position in time and space, was the same true of his view of God? If man's ordinary experiences could be analysed and their dynamics determined scientifically, could his religious experience be treated in the same way? If history was all of a piece, what place was there for any particular divine intervention? And if every culture had its own religious system, what kind of criterion could be applied to determine whether any one of these religious forms was to be preferred to any other?

These were some of the questions which were becoming insistent at the beginning of the twentieth century. More specifically they could be reduced to two major enquiries: (*a*) Is there any distinctive pattern of human experience and expression that can legitimately be called *religious*? and (*b*) If such a pattern can be defined, what is the further distinguishing mark of the particular religious experience which can rightly be called *Christian*?

These questions, indeed, were not entirely new. Schleiermacher had wrestled with them a century earlier and answered the first in terms of a feeling of absolute dependence, the second in terms of a continuity of transmission through the Christian community. Other solutions were advocated during the course of the nineteenth century. In the main the general experience was defined as an unlimited or unconditional extension of some recognizable human sensitivity, while the particular was defined first by examining the gospel-portrait of Jesus and then by claiming that the ideal manifested in and through his humanity could, by the operation of supernatural grace, be re-manifested, at least in part, in the lives of those who committed themselves to him as disciples.

But increasing knowledge of the varieties of human experience as observed and described both by artists such as the novelist and the dramatist, and by scientists such as the psychologist and the sociologist, made it increasingly difficult to single out any one form as being exclusively religious. At the same time, increasing knowledge of the world's religions made it uncertain how far what had hitherto been classified as specifically Christian could be paralleled in the experience of the devotees of other gods. For example, was not the *bhakti* experience of a devout Hindu extraordinarily similar to the *agapē* experience of a Christian saint?

The twentieth century has witnessed a massive dismissal of religion as illusion or delusion. Psychologically it has been reduced to fantasy or regarded as the product of wish-fulfilment or the projection of infantile fears. Sociologically it has been explained as the bolstering up of class domination or as compensation for class subjection. Philosophically it has been rejected as meaningless because of its inherent incapacity to submit its claims to ordinary tests of verifiability. But even apart from these more sophisticated dismissals there has been a growing tendency to discount and ignore religion because it seems to be so little related to the pursuit of health, power, affluence, pleasure – the dominant concerns of twentieth-century man.

Amongst those who, in face of these criticisms, retain their conviction that there is a facet of human experience which can justifiably be described as religious, there has tended to be a division: between those who see no need to identify this experience with specifically Christian traditions or values and those who regard the Christ-event as the crown or the criterion of all religion. The former seek a religion which is open and expansive and universal in character: the latter one which is concrete and intensive and expressed in a particular form. The former strives towards fulfilment, the latter towards commitment.

I have put forward these sweeping generalizations as a provisional hypothesis. To test them I propose to look at the careers of five pairs of men, all eminent in some department of the arts or the sciences. In the case of each pair there has been the sharing of a common interest and a common discipline; yet in the case of religion, and the interpretation of religious experience, there has been a contrast such as I have briefly described in the previous paragraph. All came to the full exercise of their powers at roughly the same time and all were educated within the context of the assumptions of Western civilization in the first quarter of the twentieth century. Is it possible to suggest what may have been responsible for their agreements and their differences? In particular, is it possible to derive from their writings insights which may help us to understand more clearly the division which exists today between those who celebrate the fulfilment of life in and through religious experience and those who through commitment to Christian faith become reconciled to God and to their fellow men and bear their witness accordingly?

I propose to compare and contrast (a) Two interpreters of universal history; (b) Two interpreters of the living world of nature; (c) Two interpreters of ordinary human experiences; (d) Two interpreters of tragic human conflicts; (e) Two interpreters of the totality of human existence.

~ 2 ~

C. H. Dodd
&
Arnold Toynbee

I

First I propose to examine the careers of two men for whom the interpretation of history was a life-long concern. C. H. Dodd grew up in Wrexham, the son of a local headmaster who was a pillar of the Independent Church in that town. During the first eighteen years of his life, he responded eagerly to the influences of home and school and chapel in all of which books and the study of language were regarded as supremely important. At home and in chapel the Bible was the centre of attention: in school the study of Greek and Latin introduced him to the world of the classics.

After gaining a scholarship to Oxford he continued his classical studies and at the same time remained loyal to the Congregationalism in which he had grown up, particularly by associating himself with Mansfield College, where in time he became a student preparing for the ministry. In his university course he leant towards history rather than towards philosophy, and after graduation set to work to equip himself for a more detailed knowledge of the ancient world by studies in numismatics, archaeology and Semitic languages. It was primarily through a mastery of languages that he hoped to capture the spirit and outlook of the inhabitants of Hellenistic and Hebraic civilizations and to understand their attitude to life and destiny.

In his religious upbringing, mysticism and sacramentalism had little or no place. Religion meant right thinking and right acting and that in effect meant thinking and acting 'according to the scriptures' (the title of one of Dodd's later books). Little stress was laid on dogmatic formulations: ethical theories commanded little interest. But in family relations, in social intercourse, and in church observances, to live according to the scriptures was the deepest concern and highest ambition of the elect community within which Dodd was nurtured before his departure to Oxford in 1902. His elders were beginning to be aware of new knowledge of the universe and of history and this needed to be reconciled with the plain statements of scripture. Yet still the authority of the Bible remained unquestioned.

As far as his approach to history was concerned, this was primarily through language – comparison, translation, interpretation. In his early environment two languages, English and Welsh, intermingled. In his church, the interpretation of the biblical text and its application to the life of society were of paramount importance. During the course of his career, he was to see major developments in the methods by which a clear and accurate translation of any text into the language of a later period could be made. Dodd, on his part, pursued a single-minded and undeviating course, a course which, as R. G. Collingwood shows in his autobiography, was regarded at Oxford as the only method of true scholarship: grapple with the text; set it in its proper context; compare it with other writings of the period; search for the central concepts and concerns of the age; finally, when the meaning of the text in its original setting seems to have become clear, transfer that meaning to the thought-forms of a later time through the medium of language which is strong, appropriate and durable. In such a view, a comprehensive facility in language is the pathway which leads to a reliable interpretation of the historical past and into a fruitful application of its lessons to the problems of contemporary life.

In his inaugural lecture at Cambridge in 1935 Dodd defined his task as follows:

> The ideal interpreter would be one who has entered into that strange first century world, has felt its whole strangeness, has sojourned in it until he has lived himself into it, thinking and feeling as one of those to whom the Gospel first came, and who will then return to our world, and give to the truth he has discerned a body out of the stuff of our own thought.

For the performance of this task a knowledge of languages, ancient and modern, was the primary necessity.

But how far does such a method lead to the construction of a comprehensive philosophy or theology of history? Can the interpretation of a particular text within its limited setting throw light upon the meaning of the total historical process? Such questions, as it seems to me, hardly arose for Dodd until much later in his career. In his days at Wrexham it would have been assumed unquestioningly that there was only one possible interpretation of universal history; that defined by the sequence creation, fall, election, redemption, the final kingdom of God. The Old Testament provided essential types and prophecies; the New Testament their critical actualization in history; the continuing experience of God's people the movement towards the consummation. What he learned in his philosophical studies at Oxford about logic and metaphysics and theories of knowledge mattered little. None of this need interfere, it seemed, with the general overall framework within which he had originally found the meaning of life. His task was to grapple with the text of the New Testament, interpret its words and concepts in the light of the most detailed knowledge obtainable of the thought-forms of surrounding cultures, and then draw out finally its central message as the clue to the meaning of all history. He would bend all his energies to showing that the purpose of God, adumbrated, foreshadowed, promised, in and through the history of Israel had in fact come to realization, to critical enactment, in the total earthly career of Jesus the Christ.

II

For the performance of this task it would be necessary, as he realized, to give the most careful attention to the views of human life and destiny expressed in the literature from Jewish and pagan circles in the centuries surrounding the birth of Christianity. It was also necessary to take account of all important researches into the way in which literary forms were generated and transmitted at that time. Dodd became expert in his mastery of the Septuagint, of the writings of the Rabbis, of Hermetic and Gnostic literature, of the Hellenism of the first century AD. At the same time he gained a thorough acquaintance with the theories of British and German scholars concerning the ways in which oral traditions were selected, combined, revised and re-shaped in written form.

Gradually the results of these labours began to appear in books. These reveal a man who, while conversant with the many and varied religions and ethical systems of the ancient world, was at the same time convinced that something utterly distinctive could be discerned amidst

6

the welter of its ideas and practices. He believed that a careful study of the Bible would bring to light 'a particular series of events in which a unique intensity of significance resides'. An historical 'event' he defined as 'an occurrence plus the interest and meaning which the occurrence possessed for the persons involved in it and by which the record is determined,' for 'in the world as we know it occurrence and meaning are inseparably united in the event'.[1] In studying the literature which belonged to the area of his special concern, he found that men's attention had been focussed upon 'a series of crises' rather than upon any kind of slow and continuous evolution. Was it not clear that these 'crises' were the result of no merely human designs and actions but rather of the direct intervention of the living God who through them manifested the nature of his total purpose to redeem mankind?

Whereas, however, the critical 'occurrence', plus the meaning attached to it by some prophetic voice, seemed in its Old Testament context provisional and preparatory, the events recorded and interpreted in the New Testament scriptures appeared to be definitive and determinative of the total destiny of mankind. Through Jesus, Dodd claimed, the 'saving purpose of God entered history at a particular moment and altered its character'.[2] His words and actions, his death and resurrection, were such as to convince the men most closely associated with these events that they represented no ordinary operation of natural forces, not even one of the crises such as had been manifested at an earlier stage in human history, but rather the unique revelation of God's kingdom, the critical actualization in time of that purpose which transcends time, the fulfilment within one particular human career of that pattern of sonship which is God's design for every member of a redeemed humanity. In these events, in fact, may be 'discerned the mighty act of the transcendent God which brings history to its fulfilment'.[3]

With unflagging and undeviating zeal, Dodd set himself the task of getting at the historical facts, while realizing always that the bare fact, the naked event, is in itself of minor interest, even if knowledge of it were attainable. Facts can be discerned only through the eyes of those who reported them. The interest and significance of events were first formulated by those who witnessed them and proclaimed them. Our task is to enter as deeply as possible into the traditions and assumptions and needs and hopes of these witnesses and then to re-interpret their testimony through the language-forms of our own time. In this task he became a trusted leader. He never shrank from the consequences of his devotion to the particular. He never lost his conviction that through

7

the testimony of the apostolic witnesses we can make contact with a real historical figure, the framework of whose human career has been reliably preserved for later generations. The meaning of that career will never be fully understood, but the career itself is sufficiently authenticated as to make it possible for us to go on believing that in and through him the living God has indeed visited and redeemed his people in a way which cannot and need not ever be repeated.

Dodd's approach to the interpretation of history, it may be noted, was almost entirely through a patient examination of texts. At an early stage in his career he worked on coins and took part in an archaeological 'dig'. But he never visited Palestine or the Middle East and never was in Greece until in his eightieth year. Words, and the events to which words bore witness: the comparison of different languages: the variations in the meaning of words in successive periods of history – these were the matters which gripped and sustained his interest. He was convinced that in the history of mankind words were of supreme importance: they were the finest instrument available for bearing witness to that Word by which the whole of human history is to be interpreted.

III

In complete contrast to Dodd's, Toynbee's early years were spent in a part of London where many belonging to the upper middle classes resided, between Paddington and Regent's Park. His father had left business to become a professional social worker under the Charity Organization Society, a philanthropic movement designed to provide supplementary benefits for hard cases ineligible for Poor Law assistance. His mother, a graduate of Newnham College, Cambridge, where she had gained first class honours in the history tripos, had been a teacher and was well qualified to inspire her son with a love of history. Toynbee had no doubt at all that it was because his mother was a dedicated historian that he elected to follow in her steps.

But in a revealing passage he once defined the way in which his own approach to history came to differ from hers. 'My mother,' he wrote 'loved the concrete facts of history for their own sake. I love them too, of course. If one did not love them one could never become an historian. I love the facts of history but not for their own sake. I love them as clues to something beyond them – as clues to the nature and meaning of the mysterious Universe in which every human being wakes to consciousness.'[4] His father was constantly concerned with the problems of human beings living in the present, his mother with the fortunes of human beings who had lived in the past. Combining these two interests, the boy developed a master passion to study human affairs, to understand the nature of the forces influencing human action, to apprehend, if he could, the ultimate spiritual reality behind the changes and chances of this mortal life and thereby to find a satisfying meaning in the whole universal scheme.

The religious atmosphere in which his formative years were spent was also very different from that of the Wrexham chapel. His parents were sincere communicant members of the Church of England. They accepted its doctrine and discipline without serious question and gained through its ministrations the sense of a supernatural grace undergirding and fulfilling their earthly lives. The pattern of Anglican ritual remained familiar to Toynbee throughout his school days and, in spite of the fact that at university he passed through a phase of agnosticism, there is little doubt that the general theological assumptions of Western Christendom retained their influence upon his interpretation of history from first to last.

Yet this influence he found in no way irreconcilable with the more obvious pattern of interpretation which governed his outlook from the beginnings of his formal education, an education which was pre-eminently an initiation into the classical age of the Graeco-Roman world. Probably no school of the time was better equipped to effect this initiation than Winchester College, of which Toynbee became a scholar. In fact he grew to be so adept in using the ancient tongues that, as he himself records, his emotions when deeply stirred always expressed themselves in Greek or Latin verse rather than in English. But, more than this, his facility in the language enabled him to explore the literature and archaeology of the classical world in a manner which few others can have equalled and in this way he came to live and move and have his spiritual being even more in that world than in the world of the early twentieth century. Its values, its standards, its interpretation of human affairs became his norms. The world which had sprung to life in the Homeric epic and had died after the delivery of the last of Demosthenes' speeches – this was to him, he said, the real world. From within this framework of discourse and behaviour he was to set about his great task of studying universal history.

What, then, was the chief consequence of choosing such a vantage-point for his survey of human relations and affairs? 'The humanist student of the Classics,' he wrote, 'is taught to see Graeco-Roman life as a unity. In his eyes the languages, literature, visual arts, religion, politics, economics and history of the Classical World are not so many separate "subjects", insulated from each other in thought-tight compartments; they are facets of a unitary way of life, and neither this nor they can be seen properly unless the parts are seen synoptically as contributions to the whole.'[5] To see life in its organic wholeness – this was Toynbee's consuming ambition. To stand within the Near Eastern world and to gaze out northwards and southwards and eastwards and westwards; to watch the rise and fall of civilizations; to trace the comings and goings of the heroic leaders of mankind; to estimate the strength of the various factors, political, economic, geographical, religious, which may have brought about revolutionary change – this came to be his task; and whatever criticisms may be levelled against the result of his labours, there can be little doubt that his *Study of History* has been one of the outstanding literary achievements of the twentieth century.

To gain his perspective, it was not enough for him to have lived for ten years in virtually daily contact with and assimilation of the literature and cartography of Greece. He felt the need of direct physical contact with the land, with its people, with customs and scenes, with wind and weather. So he became an explorer, tramping from place to place in Italy and Greece with rucksack, water bottle, and rain coat and nothing more. He met and talked with twentieth-century Greeks, descendants of the classical heroes whose literary remains he had studied with so much care and enthusiasm. So the history of the past became alive through the present and the totality of Greek culture became the very grammar of his own interpretation of human affairs.

In this interpretation religion obviously had an important part to play. The Greeks were by nature religious; they guarded their sacred places, built splendid temples, observed special days and seasons, performed ritual dramas and appointed priestly mediators. It was a religion intimately related to the total life cycle of the natural order – the regular movements of sun, moon and stars; the dying and rising again of plant life; the process of fertility in the fold and in the home; birth and death as constantly experienced in the life of the community. It was a religion concerned also with the transcending of these seemingly immutable natural processes: through imagined ascents to the changeless life of spirit, through an approximation to perfect form in a sacred building, through human acts of self-sacrifice designed to achieve some higher value.

This type of religious outlook captivated Toynbee as he identified himself with the total culture of Greece. And indeed it was not necessarily irreconcilable with the type of religion in which he had been nurtured at home and in school. Anglicanism has on the whole laid more emphasis on the Greek than on the Hebraic strands in its Christian heritage. The very genius of Anglicanism has been like that of Greek culture, organic, comprehensive, related to the total life of the community. Hence the moderate, structured Anglicanism within which Toynbee had been nurtured seemed in countless ways consonant with the religious outlook characteristic of the culture of Greece with which he became familiar.

But there was one major difficulty, so comparable to that which proved a stumbling block for St Augustine in his pre-Catholic, Platonist career. It was that the Christian church, in its formulated creeds, appeared to confess belief in an actual physical birth not dependent upon the agency of a human father, in an actual physical resurrection of a human body and its ascension into a quasi-physical heaven. 'Among the fundamental tenets of my ancestral religion,' Toynbee wrote, 'the Virgin Birth of Jesus, his Resurrection and his Ascension are incredible for me because I cannot reconcile these tenets with my mental picture of the nature of the Universe.'[6] On the other hand, he did not hesitate to affirm that

> Christianity's fundamental tenet is, as I see it, a belief that self-sacrificing love is both the best and the most powerful of all the spiritual impulses that are known to us. I believe that this is true, and I also believe that the grasp of this truth is the essence of Christianity; but my holding of this essential Christian belief does not make me a Christian; for Christianity is the religion of the Christian Church, and the Church is an institution.[7]

What Toynbee wanted, in fact, as he looked out from his Hellenic vantage point, was a religion which is ecumenical, organic, aspiring towards that which transcends man's fullest knowledge and highest earthly hopes: a religion which yields its uttermost devotion to a divine love which transfigures human beings: a religion which celebrates the constant manifestation of that love in the form of self-sacrifice, both in art and in life. It is a religion which denies all claims to exclusiveness, claims which have, Toynbee believed, disfigured every one of the so-called higher religions of mankind. It is a religion which does not seek to escape from or passively submit to the stark realities of suffering and death. Rather it is a religion which gathers them up and transfigures them within constant experiences of renewal and regeneration.

IV

To demonstrate the potential pre-eminence of such a religion, Toynbee set himself to survey not simply the records of the Near Eastern world within which Christianity made its appearance, but also the histories of all the great civilizations known to us. What could be learned about the place of religion in human life by comparing one civilization with another: the nature of each one's genesis, the dynamics of its growth, its vicissitudes, its decline and fall? Were any obvious patterns discernible in the overall development of human history? How far were these related to environmental conditions, to struggles with fellow-men, to ideological factors? It was essential, he believed, to gain some perspective of the whole if lessons were to be learned about the function and significance of the individual unit within the whole. If it could be seen that religion had played a distinctive part in the rise and fall of all known civilizations, it would then be legitimate to draw conclusions about the role which a new ecumenical faith might occupy in a civilization showing signs of disintegration and decay. This was in fact the condition, he believed, of Western civilization in our contemporary world.

The general results of his survey are well known. He claimed to be able to see in the history of every civilization a period of growth, during which it came to terms successfully with challenges of various kinds. This growth could in principle continue indefinitely, but in one case after another some challenge proved to be excessive. A period of disintegration ensued during which a creative minority emerged and this constituted the only hope for the future. This minority was normally possessed by some religious faith and it was this possession which enabled it to become the chrysalis out of which a new life came to birth. In other words, it appeared evident that human history moves according to a perceptible pattern. This pattern is not strictly evolutionary or cyclic or organic. There is place for individual variations and eccentricities. But the pulsating movement of challenge and response never ceases. Sometimes the challenge may be too severe and this leads to some kind of social collapse. But in general 'The greater the challenge, the greater the stimulus': this is the overriding law of history and of life. And even when faced with the greatest challenge of all – death in its many varied forms – it is still possible for man to confront it positively and believe that in and through the death of some element or aspect of the material order a richer and more creative life in the spirit will come to birth.

It is hardly possible to read Toynbee for long without becoming aware of the depth of his involvement in the cultural heritage which stems from Greek sources. The ancient Greek polarity between the spiritual and the material, the divine and the human, is accepted unquestioningly. One of his constantly recurring terms is the 'spiritual presence' behind (or beyond or above) the universe. Sometimes he described this presence as supra-personal and inferred that personal individuality depends upon being separated from this supra-personal reality and then at death is re-absorbed into it. All history, according to this theory, is concerned with the transcending of the material and with the re-attaining of the spiritual. Every challenge that man encounters is in fact a challenge to rise, to rise above the threat, the opposition, the ruggedness of the material environment – to rise upwards into a new experience of the spiritual which is his true home and the authentic level of ultimate reality. Whereas in the earlier volumes of *A Study of History*[8] it seemed that the pre-eminence, even the uniqueness, of the Christ who had plunged into the river of death and emerged again on the farther side was acknowledged, this celebration of the one is less obvious in his later writings. Self-sacrifice becomes the creative principle within universal history: its realization in the career of Jesus the Christ ceases to occupy the central position within his interpretation of the place of religion in history.

In his later assessments of the human situation Toynbee re-emphasized the role of religion in the record of man's historical development. Religion, he claimed, is a built-in feature of human nature.

A human being may believe sincerely that he has no religion but in moments of crisis his religion will assert itself. When he is confronted with his own imminent death, or when he is afflicted with bereavement, disappointment, self-reproach or any other form of acute spiritual suffering, he will find himself living, even if only for a moment, on the spiritual plane which he has tried to dismiss as illusion. I therefore feel certain that there is a future for religious belief. So for me, the question is: What kind of religion is likely to prevail in the future for so far as we can see ahead?[9]

As he tried to answer his own question Toynbee postulated three stages in the history of religion. The first was a reverence and respect for nature: nature-worship. The second was the worship of human power – Pharaoh or Caesar, a state or a nation, scientific or technological achievements. The third kind of religion he defined as a direct approach to the spiritual presence behind the universe and he included within this category all the so-called 'higher' religions. Each has in some way recognized the ultimate worth of 'self-abnegation, self-denial, and also if need be self-sacrifice'. If these religions can rid themselves of non-essentials and perversions and concentrate their worshippers' devotion upon these highest of all values then they may – indeed will – achieve some kind of rejuvenation and regain the ground they have lost. Not the worship of human power but the worship of love is the one and only way by which the survival of mankind can be assured and man himself saved from his animality and raised to his proper level of existence – to life in the Spirit.

It would not be difficult to criticize this schema, psychologically and sociologically. It is highly questionable whether it could to any degree be substantiated by appeal to detailed historical evidence. Yet it is a framework of interpretation which illuminates certain aspects of the human situation. Much depends on the meaning attached to the word 'religious'. For Toynbee, deeply influenced as he was by his Greek heritage, 'religion' can stand it seems for any movement of the individual psyche away from sheer physical concerns – eating, drinking, excreting, copulating, exploring – up towards 'higher' activities – thinking, contemplating, creating, organizing, worshipping. This leads him to establish a hierarchy of 'religions', with nature-worship occupying the lowest rung of the ladder and a religion of pure altruistic love the highest. Man can only fulfil himself, can only survive as a species, if he continues to ascend, individually and corporately, towards what he calls 'a religion of the highest kind'. In short 'religion' is any and every expression of man's awareness of a 'spiritual' presence behind or above his universe. Religion can be muted or corrupted but this awareness will never finally be lost. The supreme hope for mankind is that true religion will gain the ascendancy and that the human race will find its unity and its fulfilment through an ever-expanding devotion to 'charity, esteem and love'.

V

I have tried in this brief survey to compare the lives and writings of two men, each of whom has made an outstanding attempt to interpret universal history in religious terms. One has, I think, focussed his attention on purpose in history, the other on pattern in history. One has, with modesty and yet with conviction, adopted the role of prophet, proclaiming that if there is indeed an overall purpose being worked out through history, if there is an end sooner or later to be attained beyond history, then it behoves men at all costs to ally themselves with that purpose and to seek that end. The other has, with more dramatic self-revelation and yet never dogmatically, adopted the role of seer, pointing out that if there is indeed a pattern observable within the historical process, if there are possibilities of human life approximating to or declining from this true norm, then it behoves men, individually and in their corporate activities, to shape their own behaviour in conformity with the pattern which through countless examples has been revealed as the only means of renewal and transfiguration.

What are the main influences which seem to have operated in bringing about these contrasting interpretations? At one stage the two men came very close to one another as they focussed their attention on the life and literature of the Graeco-Roman world. But prior to that one boy was growing up in an environment where a certain distinctiveness, a certain *exclusiveness*, mattered intensely; where a particular community was constituted by its belief that it had been called and chosen by God to fulfill a particular mission; where in family life there was a grave sense of living under authority, an authority whose rules for life and conduct had been sufficiently declared through a particular sacred book, an authority whose sacramental presence was made manifest supremely through the gifts and demands of a particular day. However much Dodd may have broadened this conception through his later ecumenical relationships, however radical he may have become in paring away what has seemed of secondary importance in the message of the book or the observance of the day, I doubt if he ever lost the sense of the supreme importance of particularity within history – a people, a day, a message, a celebration, above all a man, a man who passed through the stages of a particular career and who in so doing realized within the actualities of space and time that final purpose towards which the whole created universe and human society are alike being directed.

But, almost at the same time, another boy was growing up in an environment where *inclusiveness* mattered. His father could move with relative ease among the members of the more affluent society above him in the social scale; at the same time he was deeply concerned to find out and alleviate the needs of the poverty-pressed society below him in the social scale. His mother bore the hall-mark of educational prestige in the England of her day; at the same time through her teaching she was concerned to make her knowledge available to those less privileged than herself. There was also the environment of London itself – heart of a great Empire politically, economically, and culturally in the early years of this century. In the young Toynbee's school life there were endless opportunities to experience, to explore, to expand. And although, as he tells us, there were emotional anxieties and personal insecurities during those formative years, he was only waiting for the moment when, achieving a new independence after his undergraduate career had been completed, he could launch out and explore to the limit the spatial contours and temporal patterns of this fascinating world. It is significant how often in his writings the word 'universe' occurs. In contrast to Dodd's particularity, we have Toynbee's universality, the first so characteristic of the Hebraic tradition, the second of the Greek.

I have tried to capture something of the quality of each of these interpreters of history. They have much in common yet finally they stand apart. Dodd himself in his book *The Bible Today*[10] turned to Toynbee's universal interpretation and found it in many ways congenial; Toynbee on his part was well aware of the importance of the particular in the midst of universal patterns. Dodd warmed especially to Toynbee's choice of the term 'transfiguration' to describe how our present historical situation may find meaning through being related to some normative pattern which can be perceived within the total phantasmagoria of human experience in time. Even so he felt constrained to find this in the particularity defined by the New Testament *kerygma* – God working out his sovereign purpose through prophetic testimony, through the historical career of the Messiah and through the operations of his Spirit for judgment and renewal in the life of the church. It is specific, founded on 'fact', focussed in the revelation made once for all through Jesus Christ, who is Lord and Saviour of men.

His treatment of the resurrection narratives is specially revealing.

Clearly something had changed these men. They said it was a meeting with Jesus. We have no evidence with which to check their claim. To propose an alternative explanation, based on some preconceived theory, is of dubious profit. What was the nature of this meeting we cannot pretend to know. What actually happened, if by that we mean what any casual observer might have witnessed, is a question that does not admit of an answer. But the events that make history do not consist of such 'bare facts'. They include the meaning the facts held for those who encountered them; and their reality is known through the observable consequence. In this instance we may be clearer about the meaning and the consequences than about the 'facts' in themselves, but this would be true of other momentous events in history. We are dealing with a truly 'historic' event. It was the culmination of previous events in the lives of these men (summed up in their memories of Jesus) and the creative starting point of a new sequence of events of which the world was soon aware.[11]

Toynbee, on the other hand, saw a universal pattern of meaning revealed through myths, through records of man's deepest psychological experiences, through the great artistic creations of mankind. There is one Greek maxim to which he returned again and again; *pathei mathos*. Man learns through suffering. Heroes of Greek tragedy, the Suffering Servant of Isaiah, Israel itself, *bodhisattvas*, saints and saviours, Jesus himself – only through willingly-accepted travail, tribulation and even death can life be transfigured and the world renewed. For Toynbee this was the crucial principle which governs the total interpretation of man's historical experience. This is, perhaps, the nearest he ever comes in his writings to particularity.

He expresses this principle in a moving passage in volume nine of his *A Study of History*. He writes that In the summer of AD 1936, in a time of physical sickness and spiritual travail he dreamed, during a spell of sleep in a wakeful night, that he was clasping the foot of the crucifix hanging over the high altar of the Abbey of Ampleforth and was hearing a voice saying to him, *Amplexus expecta* (cling and wait). He was on his way back to religion but, as he goes on to explain, he could not return to a traditional institutional form of Christianity. Yet how could a new and revived form come into being? 'If Christianity was to be re-quickened,' he continues, 'this palingenesia could be achieved only through suffering; and suffering is an experience that takes Time – and takes it at a length which is proportionate to the measure of the chastening that is required for the sufferer's salvation.'[12] He must cling and wait, letting suffering or chastening do its unhurrying work, until in the fullness of time he could receive a new power through the anguish of being born of the spirit.

How deeply Christian this all sounds! Yet so far as I know Toynbee never identified himself with any formal Christian institution. Dodd, though often I suspect uncomfortable within his ancestral framework, clung to it loyally, believing that through a particular people God's historical purpose is being worked out; Toynbee, though uncomfortable outside the Christian community, clung to the universal symbol of renewal through suffering, waiting for some new institutional embodiment to be born. And these two men represent, in many respects, the great division and great dilemma of contemporary Christianity within our Western world.

— 3 —

C. E. Raven
&
Julian Huxley

In the last years of the nineteenth century new scientific ideas began to
arouse popular interest. Slowly they gained a place within the curri-
culum of higher education. A distinguished headmaster of a public
school – Percival of Clifton – was a pioneer in establishing a science
laboratory amongst his classrooms. Dodd once recalled how, when
walking with his father on the moors one Good Friday in about the
year 1896, the conversation amongst his elders turned to 'this evolution
that they talk about'; could it be reconciled with the teaching of Holy
Writ? Throughout the nineteenth century, of course, scientific observation and experimentation had been practised in limited circles, and
remarkable advances had been made in technological inventions. But
only now, at the end of the century, were the implications of the new
knowledge beginning to receive wider attention in Britain.

I

It was in this period that the two men whose careers I am examining
in this chapter grew up. Their early experiences were in many ways
similar. Charles Raven, born in 1885, belonged to a family of the upper
middle classes living in the area of London not far from Kensington
Gardens and Hyde Park. His father had been born in New Zealand but
had been brought back to England for his public school and university

education. Though he gained no special distinction academically, he possessed a great love of Latin and a good facility for teaching it. This meant that his son, at the age of seven, was already being drilled in Latin words and constructions and the influence on his own future use of language proved to be incalculable. The mother had come to London from Lancashire where she had lived on a comfortable country estate and had developed a deep love of nature and of painting. So from his earliest days Charles was encouraged to watch, keenly and patiently, the appearance and growth of all living things and to preserve his impressions by drawing and painting and naming and later by photography.

The other boy, Julian Huxley, born in 1887, was the son of a schoolmaster teaching at Charterhouse in Surrey. The countryside near the North Downs is one of the most attractive in the vicinity of London and this was especially so at the beginning of this century before the coming of motor traffic. Here for the first thirteen years of his life Julian revelled in the sights and sounds of the natural world and enjoyed an almost idyllic boyhood. His father, he records, was a kindly man, an excellent teacher, a careful writer. Perhaps his greatest distinction was to have written the biography of his own famous father, T. H. Huxley. Evidently the story of the life and achievements of this remarkable surgeon – naturalist, painter, writer, anthropologist, freethinker – proved to be a formative influence on the young grandson, who was devoted to him during the few years in which he knew him before his death in 1895.

Yet, as in the case of Raven, the major influence on the growing boy was that of his mother. Granddaughter of Thomas Arnold and niece of Matthew, she had been one of the first women to be admitted to the new Somerville College at Oxford. Not surprisingly she loved literature and all natural beauty and became one of the most distinguished teachers of her time. But before founding what became a flourishing girls' school, she devoted herself to the education of her three boys, two of whom were to attain both literary and scientific eminence. Julian, best known as a scientist, was also both poet and writer; Aldous his brother, best known as a novelist, was in his own way a pioneer in scientific exploration. Each was nurtured in a family tradition and atmosphere where to observe the beauty of plant life and the behaviour of birds was a source of constant wonder, while to listen to fable and poetry brought endless delight.

Although Raven and Huxley both grew up in what could seem almost ideal surroundings, the time came when examination anxiety began to invade their lives. However, each achieved success, Charles proceeding to Uppingham, a school of old foundation which had sprung to a new fame in the mid-nineteenth century, and Julian to Eton, the most famous school of all. Though the choice of school may have been determined by family connections, it probably had far-reaching consequences. Charles entered school with a classical scholarship and, with no obvious possibility of developing his scientific interests academically, remained firmly enclosed within the classical discipline to the end of his undergraduate career. Julian, on the other hand, though beginning within the regular regime of classical and humane studies, was allowed to take a scientific subject as an extra, Eton having (partly through the insistence of the great T. H. Huxley) built science laboratories and made provision for the teaching of biology. When the time came to enter university, Julian obtained the zoology scholarship at Balliol and his career as scientist was virtually assured.

Beyond their intellectual and emotional development, what evidence is there of any awakening religious sensibility? Raven's grandfather, an Anglican clergyman, had possessed a strong enough conviction to take him to New Zealand as an early missionary. His son, Raven's father, was sent back to one of the Woodard Schools, founded to promote the ideals of the Oxford Movement. But he seems to have reacted against this type of religious expression and to have settled for little more than a formal Anglican allegiance. Raven's mother, however, was active in the life of her London parish church and in due course the boy was introduced to its services. The immediate effect, however, was disastrous. A children's sermon on heaven and hell so shocked the young boy that it took years for the balance to be restored. He was prepared to reverence a God who had made the wonderful world of birds and butterflies and flowers; he rejected almost passionately the image of God which the curate had portrayed. No doubt there were mollifications as he learned the Christian verities at home and in school. But it was not until the end of his undergraduate career that religious issues came to assume serious importance in his life.

Huxley's experience was different. His grandfather had been a religious rebel and had actually coined the word 'agnostic' to describe his own state of mind. Yet his father's position in a great public school must have involved at least a formal adherence to the Anglican discipline It was from his mother, however, that his earliest religious promptings were derived. 'She had,' he wrote, 'a deep sense of religion – not orthodox Christianity, but rather a pantheistic trust in the essential goodness of the universe, coupled with a sense of wonder. This sense of wonder I have inherited.'[1] This inheritance, he went on to say, had on numerous occasions risen to a summit of ecstasy – in School Yard at Eton, for example, when on a clear night he looked at the stars and felt that he could in some way possess even their immensity; or on another night when he had a strange cosmic vision and felt he could embrace the whole contents of the earth; still again during a great thanksgiving Mass in San Marco at Venice. What some might call a cosmic mysticism brought him frequent refreshment within his dominantly scientific career.

II

In 1907 Raven gained a first class degree in the Classical Tripos at Cambridge. What was he to do next? The way was open for him to pursue further study in some other subject, but what could it be? He was deeply interested in a disciplined exploration of the natural order with which he had already become familiar. But academically he had nothing to offer in this field. On the other hand, classics was an admirable preparation for theology as then taught in the university. He had an excellent equipment for the reading of the New Testament and the Fathers in the original languages. He had a good knowledge of the history of the Graeco-Roman world. And in a general way religious life at Cambridge was strong; to read theology was a respectable thing to do.

So he began his new studies in earnest. But with so much of the preliminary work already done, he determined to devote some of his time to the study of biology and specially of genetics, using the laboratory facilities which were readily available. Thus, during the extra year at Cambridge, theology and science went hand in hand and at the end his reward was a first class in theology as well as a limited, though authentic, training in the discipline of scientific enquiry. The desire to draw the two disciplines together, and to awaken in the church a proper attention to the implications of the onward march of science, became the compelling motivation of his career.

But first he had to discover a clearer vocation, a cause to which his own life could be dedicated. It was open to him to proceed to Germany for further theological study but instead he made what seemed at the time a surprising decision. He accepted a position in the local education offices of a great commercial and industrial city – the city of Liverpool. There he learned not only to submit to the daily routine of a dull job, but also to gain first-hand acquaintance with squalid social environments and to appreciate the heroic struggles of those who were seeking to bring some hope of better things into the midst of poverty and distress. In a remarkable way the presence of Christ became real to him in the mean streets of Liverpool and even more in the company of an old college friend who was burning himself out in a mission of redemption in a smaller industrial town not far away. The upshot was that what had been studied largely theoretically now became the dynamic of a living experience. He determined to dedicate himself to Christ in the service of the church in whatever way seemed best. Before the end of the critical year at Liverpool, an unexpected call came from Cambridge to return to Emmanuel College as Dean of Chapel and director of theological studies. He was ordained at the end of 1908 and, until war came, was engaged in teaching, in the pastoral care of undergraduates, and in research in patristic literature.

Huxley's interests at Oxford, like Raven's at Cambridge, were not confined to his special subject of study. He enjoyed music and poetry and, in 1908, distinguished himself by winning the Newdigate Prize for an English poem (money which he spent on purchasing a microscope). But his major task was the study of protozoa and marine biology, embryology and anatomy, and in due course a first class honours degree assured him of a secure position, if he so desired, in what was in the England of that period a very limited field. A year of research at Naples, followed by two years of teaching at Balliol, led to his appointment, at the early age of twenty-five, to the Chair of Biology at the Rice Institute in Houston, Texas. From then onwards research, teaching, lecturing, writing, organizing, in many parts of the world, all in the realm of plant and bird and animal life, occupied his astonishingly varied career. In spite of sorrows, setbacks, and nervous depressions, he succeeded in making notable contributions to biological and zoological studies and at the same time did much to improve social conditions by directing scientific knowledge to the service of mankind.

In trying to estimate the central motivation of his labours, I turn to a passage in his autobiography in which he recalls an occasion soon after his graduation in 1909. He had been invited to Cambridge to participate in the celebration of the centenary of Charles Darwin's birth. It was also the fiftieth anniversary of the publication of *The Origin of Species* and it was altogether appropriate that a representative of the Huxley family should be present. In a striking paragraph, he summarizes his own feelings at the time:

I thought of my grandfather defending Darwin against Bishop Wilberforce, of the slow acceptance of Darwin's views in face of religious prejudice, and realized more fully than ever that Darwin's theory of evolution by natural selection had emerged as one of the great liberating concepts of science, freeing man from cramping myths and dogma, achieving for life the same sort of illuminating synthesis that Newton had provided for inanimate nature. I resolved that all my scientific studies would be undertaken in a Darwinian spirit and that my major work would be concerned with evolution, in nature and in man. This was not so much a turning-point in my career as a crystallization of my ideas, a clear vision and inspiration which I can truly say remained with me all through my life.[2]

To set men free from false and superstitious ideas and to lead them towards what he conceived to be their true destiny was Huxley's dominant concern throughout his career.

III

Having brought each man to the point where he launched out on his life's work, I want now to look at the religious framework within which each set about his task. It is abundantly clear that each possessed a fine intellect, a catholic interest, a passionate love of the world of nature, a genuine desire to help his fellow-men. Raven, like Huxley, had eagerly embraced an evolutionary interpretation of the universe and believed that this new understanding of the natural order could, if grasped and accepted, direct mankind forward along the pathway of illumination and true progress. Each regarded certain types of religious belief and behaviour as obstacles to human development. Each wished in his own way to promote a new reformation of religion in the world. Each was convinced that the new scientific outlook could help to stimulate such a reformation. How then did they differ in their respective manifestoes, setting out the way in which this reformation could be achieved?

In the first place there was one conviction which they held in common. From his earliest years each was fascinated, almost awe-struck, by the wonder of life itself. In their view the mystery of life, in all its manifestations, far surpassed the mechanical structures of the universe with their reflections in man's technological achievements. Whatever the ultimate secret of life might be, no part of its self-expression was too small or too commonplace to be investigated, recorded, classified.

Moreover, each was convinced that all the several parts were constituent elements within a vital integrating process, a process which could best be described by the word which had established itself in the nineteenth century, namely evolution. To apprehend and comprehend the evolution of living things within an evolving universe was for each man the task of a lifetime. And it is significant that in spite of their differences of interpretation (to which I shall immediately refer), they gladly joined hands in their later years to do homage to Teilhard de Chardin who seemed to them to have discovered a model, and developed a language, worthy of the great life-mystery that he attempted to describe.

The second obvious fact – and herein lies a major difference between the two – is that whereas Raven at an early stage of his career committed himself to faith in God as personal and to faith in Christ as 'the mystery or illuminating event by which the nature of reality was unveiled and the meaning of evolution declared',[3] Huxley consistently disbelieved 'in a personal God in any sense in which that phrase is ordinarily used'[4] and saw no reason to accord to Jesus of Nazareth uniqueness, either of place or function in the religious evolution of mankind.

It is true that Huxley possessed a remarkable knowledge of music and literature, much of which, as he would have admitted, came to birth within the Christian ambience and as a result of what might be called Christian inspiration. But from his earliest years he lived within an atmosphere of non-dogmatic and non-institutional religion and, for a while, was attracted to a purely rationalistic humanism such as was being advocated in certain influential circles at the end of the nineteenth century. Yet out of a deep experience of conflict and frustration at the age of twenty-five, when it seemed that everything worthwhile – love and beauty and moral aspiration – had been lost, he emerged with a new religious sensitivity and a desire to join in the task which Lord Morley had defined as the next great task of science – 'to create a religion for humanity'. So in 1927 he bent all his energies to the production of a book which has since become famous, *Religion without Revelation*. Set within an evolutionary framework, it rejects any idea of special revelation, whether through divine action or through the incarnation of the personal divine. In Huxley's own words, it is a system of religious humanism without belief in a personal God.

The leading note in his interpretation of religion is what he calls 'the sense of the sacred'. Man, he believed, has an innate capacity for experiencing this sense of the sacred as he relates himself to certain objects, events and ideas. It expresses itself in and through a mixture of emotional attitudes – awe, reverence, wonder, fear, admiration: 'mystery may probably be regarded as its real essence, with awe as necessary and reverence as common ingredient'.[5] It reveals itself also in varying degrees: some experience the sense of the sacred overwhelmingly, others far less intensely, some dimly or not at all (afflicted by a kind of religious colour-blindness). But the hope of the future is for a steady expansion of this sense of the sacred, its cultivation and its satisfaction.

> I feel that any religion of the future must have as its basis the con-
> sciousness of sanctity in existence – in common things, in events of
> human life, in the gradually-comprehended interlocking whole
> revealed to human desire for knowledge, in the benedictions of
> beauty and love, in the catharsis, the sacred purging, of the moral
> drama in which character is pitted against fate and even deepest
> tragedy may uplift the mind.[6]

He was not content to wait for such a religion to develop by processes of natural selection and survival of the fittest. He believed that
religion can be organized by bringing 'the different ideas and aspirations, the goals and springs of conduct in inter-relation with each other
and with a full experience of outer reality in the widest possible way'.
He had a passion for unity and comprehensiveness. The whole personality of the individual must be related to the rest of the universe in
reverence and love.

Interestingly, Huxley believed that his own interpretation of religion
is in fact 'a retranslation of the realities at the base of orthodox Christianity into modern terms'.[7] He appealed to the Trinitarian formula of
the Council of Nicaea and attempted to show that behind the formula
there is a witness to a threefold character of reality such as he was ready
to accept. This led him to engage in an exercise of demythologization
and depersonalization, identifying the first hypostasis of the Trinity
with the powers of non-human nature, the third with the values, ideals,
aspirations constantly manifesting and re-manifesting themselves
within human nature, the second with living human beings who mediate between ideal and actual, infinite and finite, the spiritual and the
material. His Trinity became Eternal Power, Pure Idea and Spirit
incarnate in Life the Mediator. All are inter-related within an organic
wholeness which is not static but is constantly evolving towards a goal
in which spirit will perfectly control the material aspects of reality.

Such a system, in his view, is entirely 'scientific', for its language and
ideas can be analysed and tested by the help of recognized scientific

disciplines. Physics and chemistry operate in the first area, psychology in the second, biology in the third. But neither of these disciplines can operate effectively in separate compartments. Each must relate itself to the other in a common movement towards that Sacred Reality which is the unifying nisus of the whole.

In a moving passage in his *Memories* he bears witness to this Reality in a more direct way.

> In spite of all my intellectual hostility to orthodox Christian dogma, the Chapel services (at Eton) gave me something valuable, and something which I obtained nowhere else in precisely the same way. Undoubtedly what I received from the services in that beautiful chapel of Henry VI was not merely beauty, but something which must be called specifically religious. But once the magic doors were opened, and my adolescence became aware of the nature and art, and indeed the whole emotional richness of the world, pure lyric poetry could arouse in me much intenser and more mystical feelings than anything in the church service; a Beethoven concerto would make the highest flights of the organ seem pale and one-sided, and other buildings were found more beautiful than the Chapel.
>
> It was none of the purely aesthetic emotions which were aroused, or not only they, but a special feeling. The mysteries which surround all the unknowns of existence were, however, divinely contained in it, and the whole was predominantly flavoured with the sense of awe and reverence.[8]

This I have called cosmic mysticism. It reveals what can only be called the religious awareness of a man who daily lived amidst the wonders of nature but still recognized that beyond his fullest apprehension there exists the mysterious sacred which inspires within him a sense of awe, wonder and final reverence.

IV

By an interesting coincidence, in the same year in which Huxley wrote *Religion without Revelation*, Raven produced the book which was probably his most original contribution to theology, *Creator Spirit*. In this he tried in a new way to synthesize the contributions of the life-sciences with those of historical theology. He had accepted *con animo* an evolutionary framework. Now the question was whether the testimonies of the apostolic and patristic writers to the central Christ-event could be reconciled with the scientific account of this apparently inexorable life-process. These testimonies, with all their variations, were unanimous in one respect – in their claim that in Jesus Christ God had visited and redeemed his people, that in Jesus Christ the eternal God had been manifested in human form. Could a place be found for such a revelation within a total evolutionary system?

Turning to his studies of ancient history, he found illuminating clues in the eighth chapter of the Epistle to the Romans and in the writings of Origen. If there was one passage of the New Testament which beyond all others became determinative for his thinking and teaching it was Romans 8.18–27, the passage which speaks of the whole creation groaning and travailing in pain with the end-purpose of bringing to birth sons of God, that is, those bearing the character and likeness of *the* Son, Jesus Christ. If evolution is concerned with the generation of a new race, the human race, then the unceasing travail of God in creation and redemption becomes meaningful. That there should have been a revelation of what I may call the end-result in the midst of time was not, he believed, inconsistent with the whole evolutionary idea.

What stands out most clearly in any comparison of the writings of Huxley and Raven, is the contrast in their attitudes to the category of the personal. In Huxley's view to talk of personality or personal freedom or personification in a scientific context is to create confusion. Science is concerned with manifest evidences which can be observed and tested. These include human attitudes and actions: they do not, in his judgment, include attitudes or actions which need to be attributed to personal agents beyond or superior to man. Man, through his attitudes and actions, reveals a sense of the sacred but this need not mean more than that man is experiencing a supreme exaltation of spirit, an upsurge of feeling which can legitimately be called religious.

In Raven's view, on the other hand, the created order and human experience are meaningless unless conceived in terms of personal purpose and personal communion. He accepted the evidence derived from modern scientific research which seems to gain coherence only within a broad evolutionary framework. But this did not prevent him from affirming that a divine purpose operates through and in the evolutionary process. He objected as strongly as Huxley would have done to any idea of a supernatural being descending from above and playing out an evolutionary drama upon the world's stage. But he had no difficulty in imagining the agonies and struggles and 'innumerable lesser Calvaries' of the creative process as constituting the steady and costly operations of the living God. The notion of the unity of creation was for him essential. 'Creation', he wrote, 'is not an act but a continuous process of which incarnation and atonement are always characteristic.'[9] The one mighty evolutionary process is to be interpreted as the manifestation of the will and purpose of the one God who operates, not by the method of irresistible power, but through the travail of suffering love.

Yet within such an interpretation what place could be found for the emergence of one who has been regarded in Christian tradition as standing in a unique relationship both to God and to his fellow-men? Raven had accepted the challenge 'What think ye of Christ?' as the title of his first published work and he never ceased to recognize that any serious Christian apologetic must make this question its primary concern. His own answer was expressed through a thorough-going re-interpretation of human personality within the evolutionary framework.

> No doubt God is in varying degrees incarnate in all His universe: but the levels and therefore the revelations differ. In that universe as we know it, human personality holds the highest place: any concept of God in terms less than those of the fullest personality will be an idolatry: for the essence of idolatry is the substitution of a lower for the highest sacrament of deity . . . in Him is the fullness of that of which all creation has a partial share, for which all creation is a preparation, to which all creation aspires. We do not honour or worship Christ the less because we regard Him as typical, representative and illuminating, not as alien, intrusive and confounding. Rather as we see Him consummating and completing the age-long world-wide purpose of Creation, His revelation takes on a new coherence, a new validity, a new majesty. He is in the true sense God's mystery, the unveiling of a reality else dimly and mistakenly apprehended.[10]

Often in his writings Raven tried to spell out in detail the nature of this 'highest' personality revealed in Jesus. He stressed the harmony, the wholeness, the perfect union with God as Son with Father, the self-giving, the paradox of goodness and severity, the many-sidedness of his character. But he confessed that for him one aspect was pre-eminent. The picture of the sufferer whose suffering redeems was sufficient proof of 'His surpassing and unique grandeur'.[11] He suffers and thereby saves. This is the highest level of manhood: this is the authentic manifestation of godhead.

It was altogether natural for Raven to complete his trinitarian system by an enthusiastic re-affirmation of the Spirit as Lord and Giver of Life. In scientific circles the concept of energy had become central and some philosophers were interpreting the whole evolution of the universe in terms of an *élan vital*, a single life-force. Raven himself was convinced that the process of evolution displayed 'a nisus towards perfection, a holistic principle'. What he was not prepared to allow, however, was that this was just a blind, impersonal, tendency, operating in a mechanical and deterministic way, allowing no room for 'new and richer forms of being'. For him the supreme manifestation of the work of the Spirit was in the transformation of individuals and in the creation of a truly personal fellowship. The word which described the highest experience we can conceive is love and it is only in and through the energy of the Spirit that this richest of all relationships becomes possible and actual in human affairs.

Raven loved to ring the changes on the trinitarian structure which he believed constituted the form of ultimate being. Father, Son, Spirit: Creator, Redeemer, Sanctifier: Revelation, Incarnation, Inspiration. This provided him with an intellectual framework within which he could carry on both his theological studies and his scientific investigations with integrity and with each discipline illuminating the other. Yet it is still open to question whether he could have presented this intellectual reconstruction with such conviction had it not been for the fact that the Christ of history, whom he had so painstakingly studied in and through the earliest literary sources, had become alive and immediately present to him in certain critical experiences which he vividly records in his own autobiography. And it is here that we find a complete contrast to Huxley. Each claimed to have enjoyed experiences which could be called mystical or ecstatic. But whereas Huxley in no way associated these special moments of exaltation with a personal presence or a personal relation, it was Raven's deepest conviction that the occasions which had meant most to him were those in which the living Christ had become a present reality, had become indeed the very centre of his universe.

Take, for example, his account of the visit to his old college friend who was curate at Stoke-on-Trent.

Liverpool has its squalid streets and I was used to slums. But for brute ugliness Stoke and its vast and dismal churchyard stand unique. My friend was ill; I wandered up to his rooms above and the grim tragedy of the place struck me cold with misery. He had loved the country and music and all beautiful things; and he was living in this hell. I found him and behold he was not alone. No other phrase will express it. Here walking with him in the midst of the furnace was Jesus; and its flames were an aureole. He had found that which together we had sought.[12]

Once more there is his account of the day in 1927 when 'the pulling together of my scientific and religious interests was accomplished and I first achieved intellectual integration and a coherent outlook'. He had been photographing gulls and observing auks on Clay Head in the Isle of Man when suddenly the whole scene became charged with meaning.

Hitherto I had exploited nature, collecting pictures and observations, using its resources for the satisfaction of my own curiosity and possessiveness. Now I knew that there was more in it than a play-ground for the children of men or a training-school for artist or scientist. Here was a world alive, transparent, sacramental; the work of God, the object of His love, the body of His indwelling. It was for me to enjoy. 'And God saw that it was good' – that is how its story begins; and 'So God loved the world' is the secret of its suffering and its redemption.[13]

V

I have tried in this chapter to compare and contrast two men, born two years apart, educated in the same general milieu, interpreting the living world of nature within the same evolutionary framework, responding eagerly, even ecstatically, to manifestations of glory and beauty within natural phenomena, exercising roles of great distinction in public affairs. But Huxley continued to call himself an agnostic whereas Raven was to the end devoted to the service of Jesus Christ, a minister of the Christian church.

The two men met from time to time and although Raven had not hesitated to criticize Huxley's position in quite severe terms in his Open Lectures at Cambridge in 1943, they remained good friends. There is an interesting letter written by Huxley to Raven in 1949 which reveals his own state of thinking at the time.

I called at Christ's when I was in Cambridge not long ago, but you were away – I should have so much enjoyed a talk with you after this considerable space of time that Unesco took out of my life. I am groping towards a new angle of approach towards things – something more unitary than the present unfortunate dualism between 'science' and 'religion', 'materialism' and 'idealism', 'rationalism' and 'mysticism' etc. etc. An approach which would include the scientific approach and method; but also the humanistic in the largest sense, as including all the properties of the human mind and spirit – art, mystical experience, love, etc. It would try to be realistic, in the sense of not idealizing things, and especially not idealizing human nature, and admitting as basic the properties and aspects of human nature which, by and large, are dealt with in the doctrine of original sin – and clearly it would have to be evolutionary ('dynamic' – 'historical' – what you will) in insisting on the unity of *process* throughout the universe as well as on the unity of material composition, in thinking in terms of trends instead of absolute or static states, utopian or otherwise, in insisting that nothing can be fully 'explained' without reference to its history and in regarding human history as a (very special!) continuation of one branch of evolutionary history. I am hoping that you with your double background of interest in man's spiritual possibilities and in the history of science, will be able to contribute to the clearing up of some of my present difficulties.[14]

The concern here expressed for a unitary approach, for inclusiveness and realism, for process and evolutionary history, found expression some twenty years later in an article which Huxley contributed to *Playboy* magazine. This is his view of the future of religion.

It is clear that the era of mutually exclusive and dogmatic religions, each claiming to be the sole repository of absolute and eternal truth, is rapidly ending. If mankind is to evolve as a whole, it must have a single set of beliefs in common, and if it is to progress, these beliefs must be self-limiting but open-ended, not rigid barriers but flexible guide lines, channeling men in the general direction of improvement and perfection – In the light of our new and comprehensive vision we must redefine religion itself. Religions are not necessarily concerned with the worship of a supernatural God or gods, or even with the supernatural at all: they are not mere superstition nor just self seeking organization, exploiting the people's superstitions and its belief in the magical powers of priests and witch doctors.

The ultimate task will be to melt down the gods and magic and all supernatural entities, into their elements of transcendence and sacred power; and then, with the aid of our new knowledge, build up these raw materials into a new religious system that will help man to achieve the destiny that our new evolutionary vision has revealed. Meanwhile we must encourage all constructive attempts at reformulating and rebuilding religion. My personal favourite is Evolutionary Humanism, but there are many others tending in the same general direction, like Yoga and Zen, ethical and meditative systems, and the cults of release through psychedelic drugs or bodily rituals.

How does this all add up? It adds up to a meaningful whole, something greater than the sum of all its parts. We need no longer be afflicted with a sense of our own insignificance and helplessness, or of the world's non-significance and meaninglessness. A purpose has been revealed to us – to steer the evolution of our planet toward improvement; and an encouragement has been given us, in the knowledge that steady evolutionary improvement has actually occurred in the past, and the assurance that it can continue in the future.[15]

The idea of 'melting down' gods, magic and supernatural entities into their basic elements of transcendence and sacred power may seem possible to a man familiar with chemical reactions but seems strange within the context of man's psychological and social development. In a still later reflection, recorded in his book *Memories 2*,[16] Huxley returned to the attack on 'all rigid dogma', 'all ethical and intellectual absolutes', 'all narcissistic self-deification, of individuals or of nations', 'all personified divinities' and expressed his final confidence in some form of humanism which bends all its energies towards 'the ever-receding goal of the improvement of the human lot'. Thus to steer the evolution of our planet towards improvement is the purpose which gives meaning and significance to human life: and this purpose presumably is expressed religiously in every movement towards worthy 'transcendence', in every focussing of the 'feeling of sacredness on fitter objects', in every truer discrimination between right and wrong. We cannot explain the mysterious urge towards 'transcendence' which finds expression in 'religious' activities. But that religion, stripped of its dogmatism and exclusiveness, should occupy a central place in man's struggle to improve his lot, he remained firmly convinced.

As is evident, Raven shared to the full Huxley's advocacy of the evolutionary model as the only one now possible for the interpretation of universal life. He shared, too, Huxley's enthusiasm for such notions as the unitary approach, the interpretation of history as process, the concentration on man in his organic structures and relationships. But when it came to the place of religion in human life, he simply could not imagine religion at its highest and best except in terms of personal communion with the personal divine. It was the personality of Jesus which had riveted his own attention and secured his unswerving allegiance. The manifestations of purpose which he saw in the universe were utterly unintelligible to him unless they were witnesses to a personal wisdom and energy. Religion without a personal God seemed either to be at a very elementary stage in its evolution or to be a contradiction in terms.

> With Jesus, as the several lines of His personality are disclosed to me, the sense grows in me that I am in the presence of the very light of the world, of a light so brilliant that I can see only part of its spectrum. He becomes for me what he was to Clement, 'the many-coloured wisdom of God', or what he was to the author of Hebrews, 'the effulgence of His glory'. And my response must be to 'walk in the light'.[17]

Many parallel testimonies could be quoted from his other writings. He gloried in the evidences which nature provides of the design which, he believed, can only be attributed to personal purpose: he gloried still more in the personality of Jesus through whom he saw personal presence being manifested in its highest form: he rejoiced in every experience of the communion of persons in true fellowship, a communion which, he believed, is the fruit of the operation of the personal Spirit of God in human life. Yet Huxley wanted to be rid of all 'personified divinities'.

No one, I think, can read Huxley's *Memories* or his *Religion without Revelation* without carrying away the impression of an utterly honest, open-minded, large-hearted man, devoted to the understanding of the universe and to the betterment of his fellow-men. Yet in Raven's writings I find something more, something hard to define. Passion? Faith? Commitment? I suppose in the last resort it is relationship with the *ultimate as personal*. In Huxley's view it was through the mediation of mind 'enthroned above matter', in Raven's view it was through the mediation of the personal Logos, that human beings could move forward in their understanding of the universe and in the attainment of their moral destiny.

～ 4 ～

Edwin Muir
&
Wallace Stevens

In the ninth decade of the nineteenth century at least four outstanding poets – William Carlos Williams, Ezra Pound, Edwin Muir and T. S. Eliot were born. Of these I choose Muir as a notable example of a man who became committed to Christian faith. But to find an example of general religious feeling I leave aside Williams and Pound, with whose poetry I have only a passing acquaintance, and invite attention instead to Wallace Stevens who was born near the end of 1879 just before the decade began. He and Muir were near enough in age to be regarded as contemporaries. Each was in fact invited to be visiting Professor of Poetry at Harvard for the year 1955–6 (Stevens had declined and Muir accepted) and by the end of January 1959 both had died.[1]

A comparison of the lives and poetic achievements of these two men, whose outward careers were in many ways so different will, I believe, shed some light on the nature of religious experience and expression.

I

Wallace Stevens was shy and reserved and only rarely spoke of his early upbringing. He was the son of a successful attorney and was born in Reading, Pennsylvania; his mother came of Dutch stock, a group of religious refugees having sought a haven of refuge in Bucks County in the year 1709. His father was a man of culture with interests in politics and painting. 'There is no better exercise,' he wrote to his son, 'than an effort to do our best to appreciate and describe to others the beauties of those things which are denied to the vision of the absent.' There was much to see in Boston and Cambridge. 'And who knows by bringing to its description your power of painting pictures in words you make it famous – and some Yankee old maid will say – it was here that Stevens stood and saw the road to distinction . . . Paint truth not always in drab clothes.'[2] His mother, formerly a school-teacher, seems to have been deeply religious; 'I remember', Stevens wrote, 'how she always read a chapter from the Bible every night to all of us when we were ready for bed.' She would play hymns on Sunday evenings: 'The Lord preserveth all them that love him' was her favourite text.

When he entered Harvard in 1897, Stevens already possessed an extraordinary command of language. In earlier letters to his mother such words as smathering, inevictable, fluctatious and chirography occur, and his descriptions of places and natural phenomena reveal a remarkable evocation of detail. In 1899 he wrote: 'Once as I looked up I saw a big, pure drop of rain slip from leaf to leaf of a clematis vine. The thought occurred to me that it was just such quick, unexpected, commonplace, specific things that poets and other observers jot down in their note-books.'[3] A keen observation of seemingly ordinary things became for him a habit and a guiding principle.

In the magnificent collection of his letters produced by Holly Stevens there are numerous interesting references to religious impressions. He delighted to slip into a church and spend a period of quiet meditation in a dark corner; something in his nature responded to the numinous atmosphere and the religious symbols. He never despised others for finding strength and solace in traditional institutional forms. Yet it was outside, in communion with nature, in the shadow of the trees where, he said, nothing human mingled with divinity, tramping through the fields and woods – it was there that he beheld 'every leaf and blade of grass revealing or rather betokening the Invisible'.

A letter written in 1902 reveals the nature of his 'religious' feelings:

Last night I spent an hour in the dark transept of St Patrick's Cathedral where I go now and then in my more lonely moods. An old argument with me is that the true religious force in the world is not the church but the world itself: the mysterious callings of Nature and our responses . . . In the cathedral I felt one presence: on the highway I felt another. Two different deities presented themselves: and though

35

I have only cloudy visions of either, yet I now feel the distinction between them. The priest in me worshipped one God at one shrine: the poet another God at another shrine. The priest worshipped Mercy and Love; the poet Beauty and Might. In the shadows of the church I could hear the prayers of men and women, in the shadows of the trees nothing human mingled with Divinity. As I sat dreaming with the Congregation I felt how the glittering altar worked on my senses stimulating and consoling them; and as I went tramping through the fields and woods I beheld every leaf and blade of grass revealing or rather betokening the Invisible.[4]

Church rituals and atmosphere could, he granted, purify a man and soften life. But for himself: 'The sun clears my spirit and an occasional sight of the sea and thinking of blue valleys and the odor of the earth.' In a letter written in 1909 he made the only extended reference known to me to the figure of Jesus.

I dropped into St John's Chapel an hour before the service and sat in the last pew and looked around. It happens that last night I read a life of Jesus and I was interested to see what symbols of that life appeared in the chapel. I think there were none at all excepting the gold cross on the altar. When you compare that poverty with the wealth of symbols, of remembrances, that were created and revered in times past, you appreciate the change that has come over the church. The church should be more than a moral institution if it is to have the influence that it should have. The space, the gloom, the quiet, mystifying and entrancing the spirit. But that is not enough – And one turns from this chapel to those built by men who felt the wonder of the life and death of Jesus – temples full of sacred images – full of the air of love and holiness – tabernacles hallowed by worship that sprang from the noble depths of men familiar with Gethsemane, familiar with Jerusalem – I do not wonder that the church is so largely a relic. Its vitality depended on its association with Palestine so to speak. – I felt a peculiar emotion in reading about John the Baptist, Bethany, Galilee, and so on because (the truth is) I had not thought about them since my days at Sunday school (when, of course, I didn't think of them at all). It was like suddenly remembering something long forgotten or else like suddenly seeing something new and strange in what had always been in my mind – Reading the life of Jesus, too, makes one distinguish the separate idea of God.

Before today I do not think I have ever realized that God was distinct from Jesus. It enlarges the matter almost beyond comprehension. People doubt the existence of Jesus – at least they doubt incidents of his life such as, say, The Ascension into Heaven after his death. But I do not understand that they deny God. I think everyone admits that in some form or other the thought makes the world sweeter – even if God be no more than the mystery of life.[5]

To celebrate the wonder and mystery of life through his poems – this was to be Stevens' highest ambition and constant delight. He would have liked, he wrote to his future wife, to spend the whole season out of doors, walking by day, reading and studying in the evenings. But the pattern of his life proved to be very different. Going forward in the normal way through Law School and Law Practice, he attained, at a relatively early age, a position of major responsibility in a Hartford insurance company and this meant that to the end of his life he fulfilled the duties of a professional man on all working days, reserving evenings and vacations for the practice of the poetic task on which his heart was set.

It is interesting to speculate on the effect that this division of time and energy may have had on his poetry. Roy Fuller, a great admirer of Stevens, makes this comment:

I wonder if it is too fanciful to suggest that Steven's long lifetime of secular sensitivity to reality was sustained by his day to day absorption in business affairs. Certainly the relations between reality and poetry to be found everywhere in his work are paralleled by the relations of his office and his evening pursuits, and I don't think the analogy necessarily glib or superficial. Many artists are, through the very success of their art, led away from the tensions and the sources that brought it into being. And absorbed in the world of art they can become a prey to idealistic notions that their earlier years in the realer world would simply have never entertained. Spot illustrations are apt to be crude but the cases of D. H. Lawrence and T. S. Eliot spring to mind. It would be absurd to say that when the former left the Midlands, and the latter Lloyds Bank, decline set in, but it can hardly be denied that what is unsatisfactory in the later careers of both writers stems from a slackening of their hold on reality and the importation into their work of ideas that we can't help but feel to be false or at the least inappropriate.[6]

It is clear enough from this comment that 'real' and 'reality' are slippery words. 'Real' can be used in a dominantly physical or material or workaday sense: all that is involved in man's work at the coal-face or at the till or in the office: what is involved in woman's work in the kitchen or in the hospital ward or at the typist's desk. It is suggested that in these contexts humans are dealing with the realities of their existence without possibilities of escape into day-dreaming or high-falutin' ideas. On the other hand, though Stevens was very aware of these kinds of 'reality', he was also very sure that they did not constitute ultimate 'Reality'. He wanted always to keep close to the physical world and to acknowledge its constraints. Yet far more importantly he wanted constantly to pass through these constraints to the world of Reality and to do this via the medium of poems which would challenge and assist hearers or readers to pierce beyond appearances and hum-drum occurrences to Reality itself. This Reality cannot be defined or enclosed in any form of words. It can only be approached, now by this poem, now by that. It is manifested through the physical world but only begins to take on form within the human imagination through the devoted labours of the true artist.

II

Edwin Muir, though sharing something of Steven's outward reserve, was prepared when the time came to explore the deepest recesses of his memories and to expose them to public view in one of the most brilli-ant accounts of childhood experiences that we possess. Published in 1940 under the title *The Story and the Fable*, the title itself indicates that the story was to be regarded not as an end in itself but as intimately related to the fable of universal human life. He knew that his own experience was but a minute element in the total experience of man-kind. Yet could it perhaps be the case that his own individual story was the particular and detailed working out, in a limited time-span, of a far more comprehensive pattern? He had begun life in an Eden; he had known the paradisial delights of the innocence of childhood; he had been torn away from the Garden and had found himself in a desolate wasteland of strife, disease, poverty and death; he had gone out like Abraham into new lands but there had encountered distrust, tyranny, despair. Was his own story just one example of the total fable of a fallen humanity?

Muir was born on a farm in one of the remotest parts of Great Britain

– the Orkney Islands. The physical surroundings are such that man can never afford to relax; long winters, uncertain summers, fierce storms, driving rain. Yet the harvests of land and sea, the produce of flocks and herds, have been sufficient to ensure a reasonable standard of living, while a strong communal spirit has manifested itself in mutual assistance in work by day and in the recital of stirring legends and ballads in the dark winter nights. Muir looked back on his childhood days with almost unalloyed pleasure. His family was united within the embrace of parents who loved and respected each other and shared a deep religious faith. With their six children they made music and sang the old folk-songs; on Sunday evenings all gathered round to hear the earthly father reading Bible stories and commending his household to the care of the Father in heaven.

In sensitive and convincing fashion Muir describes the character of the environment in which they all lived. The land, the house, the animals, the community itself were all held together by invisible bonds linking them to the over-arching sky; under its vast dome order and harmony seemed assured. Furthermore, all that existed in the island home seemed unaffected by time; childhood already brought intimations of immortality. This was his Eden, secure, timeless, lit up by moments of dazzling splendour, which in later years he recaptured in his poetry.

But if the original experience was suffused with splendour and light, the succeeding years, from the age of six onwards, brought him into an ever-darkening gloom. He and his family seemed to have been expelled from Paradise. He passed through periods of ill-health and unhappiness in school; the family began to break up when they were compelled to leave the farm; in his fifteenth year the final blow fell – his parents moved to Glasgow and he found himself in the midst of some of the worst slums and most miserable working conditions of any city in Britain. Not that he actually lived in the slums, but his daily journeys to and from work brought him face to face with what he described as 'crumbling houses, twisted faces, obscene words heard casually in passing, the stench of pollution and decay, a great spreading swamp into which I might sink for good'.

Still worse was to follow. Soon his father died, one brother succumbed to TB, another endured the slow agony of a brain tumour, and then came the death of his mother. Meanwhile he struggled on with a variety of poorly-paid jobs, one of which in a bone-factory outside Glasgow brought a sensitive soul as near to the horrors of Gehenna as could be imagined. But he refused to capitulate and began to make friends with those of his own age who were interested in politics and literature. He was attracted to socialism, read Nietzsche exhaustively, tried his hand at writing for journals, identified himself with secular movements concerned for social uplift. Yet he was unsatisfied, uncertain of himself, unfulfilled.

Then in 1918 the turning point came. He met and married Willa Anderson, a remarkably cultured woman who was to be his brave companion to the end of his journey. Through her deep understanding and sympathy, through submitting for a period to a course of psychoanalysis, through the stimulus of a new career in central Europe learning languages, writing and translating, he gradually gained a new stability. With renewed confidence in the present and fresh hope for the future he was ready to retrace his steps into the past, to confront those forces which had so twisted and tangled his life, ready to seek a meaning in it all which would not only satisfy his own mind but which might also bring hope and encouragement to other wrestlers with the problems of ordinary life.

So when he was thirty-five years of age he began to write poetry in earnest, drawing upon dreams, fantasies and memories of his own, upon the great stories of the Bible and of ancient mythology, and upon his awareness of political movements in the world around him which were heading towards disaster in Austria and Prague. But it took him a long time to perfect his technique and to bring his strange medley of impressions and insights under control. From 1934, however, books of poems were published at fairly regular intervals and when, in 1958, a complete collection was issued it was clear that he deserved a place among the major poets of his time. There is nothing flamboyant in his poetry, no startling innovations in technique, no unusual manipulations of language. Rather there is depth – depth of sincerity, depth of feeling; there is concern – concern for his own self-understanding, concern for the health of society at large. There is great originality, it seems to me, in his handling of images drawn from dreams and from ancient mythologies and in his symbolic representations of the needs and conflicts of the human psyche. In short, if Tillich's definition of religion as ultimate concern is in any way valid, then Edwin Muir was already expressing through his early poetry a deeply religious attitude to life. Of his explicit religious affirmations more will need to be said. But the whole approach to life and experience implicit in his poetry is such as to mark him out unmistakably as a man of honesty and humility who was ever seeking to celebrate the ultimate meaning of human existence in face of the appalling evil that he had seen and known.

III

The outward aspects of Muir's religious development are not hard to trace. Nurtured in the strict Calvinism of Knox and Melville, worshipping in the kirk crowning the barren brae from which he heard the seagull's scream, he had been deprived of the concrete imagery of the Word made flesh; in later years he looked back on it all as abstract, cold and impersonal, a weaving of words within words which starved the imagination of the growing boy. Even so it had made him familiar with the biblical interpretation of history and although he yielded himself for brief periods to the subtle attractions of Nietzsche and Marx, and even of the Apostle of Social Credit, he could find no abiding satisfaction in any schemes of a purely secular kind. Then, in 1939, at a time of special anxiety, there came to him a remarkable experience which impresses by its very simplicity and naturalness. He had seen children one afternoon playing marbles, a game whose appropriate season had come round again in their annual cycle. Here was a symbol of life's renewal, a constantly re-enacted resurrection. And that night, he tells us, undressing for bed, he found himself 'reciting the Lord's Prayer in a loud emphatic voice – a thing I had not done for many years – with deep urgency and profound disturbed emotion . . . As I repeated the prayer over and over, meaning after meaning sprang from it, overcoming me with joyful surprise, and I realized that this simple petition was always universal and inexhaustible, and day by day sanctified human life.'[7]

In this moment of revelation the outline of the world's fable suddenly took visible shape. He saw Christ as the turning-point of time and the meaning of universal history. He saw him as the Incarnate One, who had taken the form and fashion of ordinary humanity and had restored the image which individuals and societies alike had lost. Some ten years later the experience gained a still more vivid clarification when he lived for a while in Rome and feasted his eyes on the artistic splendours of Christian history. He saw the image of God Incarnate everywhere and gained a deeper conviction that One had indeed assumed the burden of our flesh, lived our life and died our death. He discovered in Italy, he writes, 'that Christ had walked on earth and also that things truly made preserve themselves through time in the first freshness of their nature. So the northern child of Calvinism was in middle age awakened to a sensuous as well as a spiritual perception of what the Mediterranean world might take for granted.' Though he could never bring himself to formal identification with a credal orthodoxy or an institutional allegiance, his poetry henceforward bore witness to the depth of his Christian conviction and to the reality of the glory which he had seen.

If there is one word beyond all others which serves to describe in summary form the new life which began for Muir in 1939 it is, I think, the word 'transfiguration'. Amongst his finest poems are those entitled 'The Transmutation' and 'The Transfiguration'. Eden and Paradise and the clear unfallen world and the radiant kingdom and the pure image of God are realities which cannot be destroyed by man's folly or fecklessness. But man is now unaware of them or sees them only brokenly and dimly. Fallen from innocence he wanders through labyrinthine ways, smoke and death and money everywhere, striving to construct his own utopian systems, struggling to overcome his rivals in the fight for survival, reeling under the blows of personal misfortune, physical suffering and agonizing grief. Such had been his own experience. The clue to life's mystery had for long eluded him. The story of his own life seemed meaningless and absurd.

But now, in the presence of Christ, with Christ giving meaning to the universal scheme of things, with Christ revealing the secret of healing and restoration, all things were transfigured. This is how he described the great transmutation in the lives of Jesus' disciples:

> we felt that virtue branch
> Through all our veins till we were whole . . .
> The source of all our seeing rinsed and cleansed
> Till earth and light and water entering there
> Gave back to us the clear unfallen world.
> > . . . Was it a vision?
> Or did we see that day the unseeable
> One glory of the everlasting world . . . ?[8]

So, backwards over his own story and over the story of the human race, Muir allowed his mind and imagination to range, noting intimations, repetitions, aspirations, hopes. He did not attempt to go beyond his own transfigured vision. Nothing can be proclaimed as certain, as absolute, as inexorably predestined. But the archetypal fable is there, representing some of the constantly repeated stages on life's journey.

And the dramatic fulfilment of the fable is to be found in the record of an annunciation, an incarnation, a cross and a resurrection.

Muir never presses the issue, never attempts to hector into belief. All he knows is that for himself, since the coming of grace in history and to his own vision, the human scene has been transfigured. Never perhaps is his conviction more firmly expressed than in his meditation on the dying Bruce thinking of his murder of Comyn.

> 'But that Christ hung upon the Cross,
>   Comyn would rot until time's end
> And bury my sin in boundless dust.
>   For there is no amend

> 'In order; yet in order run
>   All things by unreturning ways.
> If Christ live not, nothing is here
>   For sorrow or for praise.'[9]

IV

I find it difficult to imagine Stevens the poet behind the big comfortable-looking figure, well-dressed, unhurried, going daily to his office in the insurance building at Hartford. There he spends the day, immersed in figures, statistics, the language of law, the abstractions of money; committees, presumably, and interviews; the dry concerns of business and commercial life. Is his imagination active during this time or does it lie dormant? That he took his professional career seriously is obvious. Was it a necessary part of his existence, if only to send the imagination reacting and rebounding with maximum velocity at the end of the day? There seems something in his career comparable to an earlier New England pattern in which men concentrated their energies during six days of the week on work in the secular city, exploring, exploiting, controlling, and then on the seventh day recoiled to a wholly different world, the world of the spirit, of another age, of grace and judgment, of origins and destiny.

Yet Stevens was insistent that reality was not to be found apart from the physical world.

'The greatest poverty', one of his finest poems asserts, 'is not to live in a physical world.' Indeed it was an essential tenet of his mature philosophy of life that reality is to be celebrated, not by attempting to ascend in imagination to a realm of being which is the kingdom of God, still less by attempting to project oneself in imagination into a future which is the kingdom of man; long before the theological developments of the 1960s Stevens was proclaiming the death of the God-idea and the impossibility of replacing it by that of a man-made utopian future. Not that he despised or repudiated the idea of God – it had, he said, been the supreme poetic idea in the history of mankind but it was no longer tenable in the world of today. Religion had been the great illusion which had sweetened and strengthened human existence. But now man must come to terms with reality in the here and now – within things, not beyond them, reflecting the energy of things in the present rather than the force driving them towards some dreamed-of future.

In a sense, then, Stevens is already the existentialist, the demythologizer, the enemy of all dogmatic formulations, the man who confronts reality alone. Again and again he refers to the poet as hero. Yet all are agreed that Stevens himself was modest, unaggressive, quiet in speech. And in one of his loveliest aphorisms he speaks of humility as the supreme virtue; it is the humble man who walks 'barefoot into reality'. He could not with sincerity utter the name of God; yet he was convinced that the world was good. Like Iris Murdoch in her volume of essays *The Sovereignty of the Good*, he added a single letter to the old integrating title of ultimate reality and wrote movingly about this good but godless world. Only, in Stevens, goodness assumed the language of beauty rather than of morality, as in Miss Murdoch's book.

What then, according to Stevens, is the role of the poet in this desacralized world? Obviously he is a craftsman in language; to weave words together into ordered patterns is now, as it always has been, his task. But he can do this only in so far as his imagination is sensitively feeling towards, probing towards, reality as it becomes immanent in the most ordinary objects and events. 'An Ordinary Evening in New Haven', 'Chocorua', 'The Man with the Blue Guitar', 'The Old Woman and the Statue' – out of chance encounters and commonplace experiences the imagination seizes material for the weaving of the fictive web of words with which reality can be clothed. The perfect poem would be identical with reality but that is beyond any man's capacity to write. His task is to capture the shape, the colour, the moment, in and through which reality expresses itself and to construct 'Notes toward a Supreme Fiction', the title of the poem which is generally regarded as Stevens' finest achievement. In his own words he would choose 'a bit of reality, actuality, the contemporaneous'. He would apply his 'sensibility to something perfectly matter-of-fact'. He would body himself forth in the figurations which make up his poem and so would mediate authentic reality to his readers.

One of his most succinct definitions of the poet and his task is I think to be found in this couplet:

> He is the transparence of the place in which
> He is and in his poems we find peace.

Transparence immediately suggests light and it is perhaps through our whole experience of light that we can come nearest to Stevens' governing concepts. Light does not create; it reveals to the eyes of men that which has been or is being created. It dances amongst things, penetrating to all the places from which it is not excluded by some impenetrable, impassable barrier. The poet is essentially the transparence, the window through whom, by means of his words, a particular place becomes iridescent. His is a tremendous responsibility. Indeed Stevens affirms that 'after one has abandoned a belief in God, poetry is the essence which takes its place as life's redemption'.

What does all this mean? Has Stevens discovered within himself the power to weave words into the most intricate and harmonious patterns in the way that the great painter operates with colours or the musician with sounds? And has he then inflated his own importance, claiming that he is now the privileged interpreter of reality? Does he now see himself as replacing the worshipper of the God who in earlier ages was regarded as the sole creator of light, in whose light alone man could see light, whose coming in the flesh brought the true light to the world, whose illuminating Spirit continually enabled men to find meaning even amidst dark and perplexing experiences? At first sight this might appear to be the case. Yet the fact remains that there is nowhere a trace of arrogance or self-opinionatedness in his writing. There is a passionate search for reality. There is an almost breath-taking achievement of beautiful forms in language, a continuous awakening of delight in the heart of the reader who responds to his gaiety.

> Natives of poverty, children of malheur
> The gaiety of language is our seigneur.

Furthermore, there is no trace of superficial optimism, no attempt to deny that there is much in the world that seems evil and painful to behold. Soldiers are wounded and die. Human love includes much sorrow. Yet he is convinced that there is an aesthetic which can even

incorporate evil, that the poet confronting reality with complete can-
dour will yet find words to express a beauty which is finally harmonious
and in which apparent contraries are reconciled. In his poem 'The Rock'
he affirms that above the cold, dark, bare descent into the earth there is
an upper surface which is green, whose leaves are for the healing of
the nations.

So this poet struggles towards the ultimate which he admits he can
never attain. He renounces the god of the single vision, the fixed
formulary, the dogmatic affirmation, the once-for-all revelation. But
does he not still bear witness to a kaleidoscopic reality which is ever
eluding man's grasp but is ever manifesting itself through the patterns
of the natural world which call forth pleasure, even ecstasy, in the
human sensibility? He denied the god of the one fixed place, of the one
fixed time, of the one particular society. He affirms a reality which is
present in the most ordinary experiences of life and whose lineaments
are represented by a never-ending succession of poetic creations. Is he
not in all this very near to affirming and celebrating the God beyond
God of Paul Tillich or the consequent God of the process-theologians?

V

I come tentatively to a final comparison between these two poets. The
career of the one was pre-eminently concerned with the tragic elements
of life; displacement, disease, disappointment, disillusionment, death.
The career of the other with what in the best sense can be called the
comedy of life; the lights and shades, the air-borne and the earth-
bound, the exciting and the dull, with the dynamism of life always
renewing its victory over the stasis of death. Muir, trying to come to
terms with his own story, a story which contained so much that was
painful and perplexing, found meaning and reconciliation by relating
his own experiences of horror and tragedy to what he called The
Fable – the world-embracing story of tragic loss recapitulated and
restored through the suffering and death of a single representative
figure in history. Stevens, trying to come to terms with his experiences
of the ordinary and the recurring in everyday life, found meaning and
beauty by allowing his imagination free rein and by gathering its
spoils into word-patterns of an astonishing variety, capable of evoking
endless pleasure and delight.

In commenting on the poetry of Muir, I referred to his titles 'The
Transmutation' and 'The Transfiguration'. Strangely enough in

Stevens' poetry also such words as transformation and transport find a place. It is the poet's task to effect a transformation by the freshness of his vision of the world; it is first to decreate reality and then to transform it by means of words and thereby to transport his hearers from a winter of discontent into a summer of delight. No one that I know has celebrated the rapturous joy of new creation more beautifully than has Stevens in his greatest poem, 'Notes toward a Supreme Fiction'.

> Two things of opposite natures seem to depend
> On one another, as a man depends
> On a woman, day on night, the imagined
>
> On the real. This is the origin of change.
> Winter and spring, cold copulars, embrace
> And forth the particulars of rapture come.[10]

The perfect poem will never be written. Always the poet is striving to approach through his language more closely to that mysterious 'presence' which is for him ultimate reality. 'Presence', as J. Hillis Miller has finely said, 'means the closeness of consciousness to itself; the proximity of the mind to its objects in the present moment, a moment which has put aside all past and future; the intimacy of language to the mind and its objects in a speech which emerges with the moment out of its hiddenness.'[11]

It is what Stevens calls in a late poem 'This *vif*, this dizzle-dazzle of being new'. The poem is entitled 'St Armorer's Church from the Outside' and is a rare example of the elaboration of a theme suggested by a traditional religious symbol. It begins by describing the ruin of what had once been a massive church: a sumac now grows on the altar. But a new chapel is in process of being built:

> a chapel of breath, an appearance made
> For a sign of meaning in the meaningless,
>
> No radiance of dead blaze, but something seen
> In a mystic eye, no sign of life but life,
> Itself, the presence of the intelligible
> In that which is created as its symbol.
>
> It is like a new account of everything old.

In vivid metaphorical language Stevens continues to celebrate the chapel as evidence of the need of each generation to be itself, to be actual as it is.

> St. Armorer's has nothing of this present,
> This *vif*, this dizzle-dazzle of being new
> And of becoming, for which the chapel spreads out
> Its arches in its vivid element,
>
> In the air of newness of that element,
> In an air of freshness, clearness, greenness, blueness,
> That which is always beginning because it is part
> Of that which is always beginning, over and over.[12]

Presumably the chapel will quickly become a 'fixture' but through his poetry Stevens tries to capture the new beginning, the living growth, the momentary revelation of reality. He does not mourn the decay of the past. The great church bore witness to reality in its own day. The chapel now takes its place.

Muir on his part, while rejoicing in the present, has no wish to disclaim the more traditional language which speaks of God and grace and the source of every human inspiration.

> As I look back on the part of the mystery which is my own life, what I am most aware of is that we receive more than we can ever give; we receive it from the past, on which we draw with every breath, but also – and this is a point of faith – from the Source of the mystery itself, by the means which religious people call Grace.[13]

And in spite of my immense admiration for Stevens, the surpassing beauty of his language, the daring flights of his imagination, the power to transform ordinary mundane things into dazzling reflections of ultimate reality, I still find greater satisfaction – more, words which express more faithfully my own deepest understanding of life's mystery – in my favourite amongst Muir's collected poems. It is entitled 'One Foot in Eden'.

> One foot in Eden still, I stand
> And look across the other land.
> The world's great day is growing late,
> Yet strange these fields that we have planted
> So long with crops of love and hate.
> Time's handiworks by time are haunted,
> And nothing now can separate
> The corn and tares compactly grown.

The armorial weed in stillness bound
About the stalk; these are our own.
Evil and good stand thick around
In the fields of charity and sin
Where we shall lead our harvest in.

Yet still from Eden springs the root
As clean as on the starting day.
Time takes the foliage and the fruit
And burns the archetypal leaf
To shapes of terror and of grief
Scattered along the winter way.
But famished field and blackened tree
Bear flowers in Eden never known.
Blossoms of grief and charity
Bloom in these darkened fields alone.
What had Eden ever to say
Of hope and faith and pity and love
Until was buried all its day
And memory found its treasure trove?
Strange blessings never in Paradise
Fall from these beclouded skies.[14]

⟬ 5 ⟭

T. S. Eliot
&
D. H. Lawrence

One of the most controversial verdicts of this century in the field of literary criticism was that of T. S. Eliot on D. H. Lawrence. Today few would question Eliot's status as 'the most influential poet of the modern English-speaking world'; on the other hand many would wish to follow Leavis in acclaiming Lawrence not only as our last great writer but as still *the* great writer of our own phase of civilization. Yet, in a review written in 1931, Eliot was prepared to dismiss Lawrence as 'ignorant' and to deliver the verdict that 'had he become a don at Cambridge his ignorance might have had frightful consequences for himself and for the world, rotten and rotting others'. In 1934 Eliot returned to the attack in his Page-Barbour Lectures delivered in the University of Virginia, though in fairness it must be added that the book containing these lectures, published under the title *After Strange Gods*, was the single volume of his collected works that he would willingly have withdrawn in later years – he refused in fact to have it reissued.

I

In spite of certain modifications in his later judgments, Eliot undoubtedly continued to find Lawrence's writings distasteful: he never ceased to regard him as a man who worked by instinct rather than by intelligence. In his earliest attacks he accused him of snobbery, sensual morbidity and intuition – 'from which he commonly drew the wrong conclusions'. In *The Idea of a Christian Society* published in 1939 he judged him less harshly:

> The struggle to recover the sense of relation to nature and to God, the recognition that even the most primitive feelings should be part of our heritage, seems to me to be the explanation and the justification of the life of D. H. Lawrence and the excuse for his aberrations.[1]

Yet in a foreword to a book on Lawrence written some ten years later, he showed that his underlying antipathy remained substantially unchanged.

> He was a man of fitful and profound insights, rather than of ratiocinative powers; and therefore he was an impatient man: he expressed some of his insights in the form least likely to make them acceptable to most of his contemporaries, and sometimes in a form which almost wilfully encouraged misunderstanding.

He believed that Lawrence constantly drew 'wrong conclusions in his conscious mind from the insights which came to him from below consciousness'. And as for his religious attitude 'we can now begin to see how much was ignorance, rather than hostility; for Lawrence was an ignorant man in the sense that he was unaware of how much he did not know'.[2]

Yet in spite of the gulf which divided these two near-contemporaries (Lawrence was born in 1885, Eliot in 1888), it is legitimate to describe both as superb dramatic artists. Lawrence was novelist, essayist, poet: Eliot was philosopher, poet, playwright. In the major works of each there is a tremendous sense of the tragedy of human life and of the dramatic situations in which both society and individuals are constantly involved. Each could write exquisitely about objects and movements in the life of nature but always, I think, with the implication that nature is the setting or the background of the drama which is actually being played out within the life of humanity. Lawrence did not often attempt to write stage-drama, but Leavis has called *Women in Love* a 'dramatic poem' and his novels have proved readily adaptable to screen production. In the case of Eliot, while there can be little doubt that his enduring fame will rest largely upon his achievements in the realm of poetry, he himself intensely desired to speak to the masses through drama and spent much of his creative energy in experimenting to this end.

In a second respect the two men had a common bond. Each had a deep concern for religion: each regarded himself as a fundamentally 'religious' man. In Eliot's case this claim would, I imagine, cause no surprise. Long before his formal commitment to Christian discipleship and church discipline, he was wrestling with religious issues. For example, he once told the Chilean poet Mistral that at the time when he wrote 'The Waste Land' he was seriously thinking of becoming a Buddhist, a not unnatural consequence of his close study of Indian religion and culture at Harvard some ten years previously. But his keen interest in other forms of religious expression – the Catholicism of the Middle Ages, the world of Dante, the ritual patterns exhibited in the writings of James Frazer and Jessie Weston – indicates that the concern for ultimacy was never far from his inner consciousness and that even in the years of non-commitment he was still an earnest seeker after some transcendent reality.

To describe Lawrence as a religious man, however, may seem an odd use of the term. Yet in a letter to Edward Garnett in 1914 he said: 'You tell me I am half a Frenchman and one eighth a Cockney. But that isn't it. I have very often the vulgarity and disagreeableness of the common people, as you say Cockney, and I may be a Frenchman. But primarily I am passionately a religious man, and my novels must be written from the depth of my religious experience. That I must keep to because I can only work like that. And my Cockneyism and commonness are only when the deep feeling doesn't find its way out, and a sort of jeer comes instead, and sentimentality and purplism. But you should see the religious, earnest, suffering man in me first, and then the flippant or common things after.'[3] The 'religious, earnest, suffering man' is a striking phrase. It might seem to fit Eliot exactly. Yet, as I have already noted, in the early 1940s Eliot seemed anxious to dissociate himself entirely from what he called Lawrence's 'heresy'. Was Eliot indeed the great pillar of orthodoxy and Lawrence the arch-heretic in matters of religion? In trying to answer this question, I propose to look back over the early environments and experiences of the two men, always remembering that so far as their pilgrimage through time was concerned, they were almost exact contemporaries.

II

I want first to direct attention to some of the factors which may have influenced Eliot's early religious development. Though home and education during the first seventeen years of his life were centred in St Louis, the traditions and atmosphere of New England were constantly affecting his unfolding consciousness. His grandfather, an eloquent preacher and brave social reformer, who had left the Harvard Divinity School in 1834 to devote his life to a ministry in the rapidly growing city of the Middle West, died in the year before he was born; but the name and fame of William Greenleaf Eliot and the principles which had governed his deep concern for man's spiritual potentialities in the midst of exploding material prosperity, must have been mediated to the grandson both by his father who, though following a business career, had remained loyal to the family traditions, and by his mother who, drawn from the same New England stock, reinforced the devotion to high thinking and right living so characteristic of the Puritan Founding Fathers.

The influence of Mrs Eliot on T.S., her seventh child, must have been far-reaching. Herself a brilliant scholar at a time when few women could enter university, she devoted herself first to teaching and later to social work. But her heart's love was for literature and poetry and probably her greatest personal satisfaction, after the birth of her children, was to see a poem of her own appearing in print. In her writing she did not neglect form but her chief ambition was to re-interpret and re-express the dramas of biblical, and, later, Christian history through poetic rhythm and imagery. She and her husband were religious conservatives, never deviating from the spiritual and moral principles of their heritage. Yet in her poetry she reveals a striking openness to the significance of more Catholic forms of worship and corporate discipline. Her young son's initiation into the world of poetry gave him at least some feeling of a wider range of religious expression than that of the Unitarian Church and household within which his earliest years were spent.

The time came when he began to yearn for a far more extensive understanding of history and human experience than the theological system of St Louis, inherited from New England, could afford. But there was another notable link with New England in his earliest years – a link which he never wished to sever and which provided him ultimately with the atmosphere and images of perhaps his finest single poem. Every summer the family went on vacation to the shore north of Boston and there the young boy revelled in the expansiveness of the ocean, the rugged splendour of the rocks and the sights and sounds of sea-faring adventure. Away from the smoke and stifling heat of the city, the relentless flow of its muddy brown river, the noise and smell of its industry, he exposed his inner being to rhythms and images which seemed to belong to another world and which were to appear years later in his deeply religious poem, 'The Dry Salvages'.

Eliot never spoke with disrespect of his early upbringing. He never disowned the firm Puritan distinction between right and wrong, between disciplined toil and momentary indulgence, though he criticized its philosophy of what constituted success as, for example, in the Introduction which he wrote for *Nightwood*:

> In the Puritan morality that I remember, it was tacitly assumed that if one was thrifty, enterprising, intelligent, practical and prudent in not violating social conventions, one ought to have a happy and 'successful' life. Failure was due to some weakness or perversity peculiar to the individual; but the decent man need have no nightmares.[4]

But he had to find his own way, to establish his own framework of reference, to explore to the limits of his ability the worlds of philosophy, literature and social structures before he could begin to express, as it proved to be through poetry, his deepest convictions and feelings concerning the universal human drama.

The range of his intellectual pursuits between his entrance to Harvard in 1906 and the completion of his doctoral thesis in 1916 is astonishing. He could have made his career in the teaching of philosophy, of comparative literature, possibly even of languages. But instead he embarked on the precarious adventure of creating poems. The disciplines which had trained him to think logically and to use words exactly were now to be superseded by a discipline which would be concerned with the transposition of ordinary thoughts and feelings into poetry.

To this end he would go on exploring and exploiting the riches of the great poetic tradition which he had inherited, and at the same time would expose himself as fully as possible to the patterns of social behaviour in the contemporary world. Both from his study of tradition and from his experience of life around him, questions about an ultimate meaning and purpose, about an ultimate framework of order, could hardly fail to arise. Certainly in tradition the religious issue had been of paramount importance. In the contemporary world the absence of religious conviction could be as significant as its presence. Though mankind at large might not be able to bear very much reality, Eliot himself could not avoid the challenge to what Leavis has called 'a sustained, heroic, and indefatigably resourceful quest of a profound sincerity of the most difficult kind'. 'The Eliot of "Hollow Men",' he goes on, 'had a desperate need to be able to believe in, to be sure of, something real, not himself, that should claim allegiance and give meaning'.[5]

How far this quest, this need, was made the more urgent by the chapter of his own domestic life which opened with his marriage in 1917 and only closed after years of suffering in 1947 it is impossible to gauge. Be that as it may, it seems clear that 1916–17 marked a decisive stage in his development. Henceforward, he was to be the interpreter of the deepest human emotions, the most tragic human experiences, through dramatic poetry. And ultimately, after years of struggle, this led him to the profoundest experience of all – to the still point of the turning world – to the timeless moment – the experience in which the human spirit becomes aware of the presence of that which can only be called divine. Furthermore, because Eliot passionately believed in the necessity for form and discipline in the ordering of all human affairs, it was natural that he should also seek to set his experiences of the divine within some kind of ordered framework. It seemed to him that a liberal Catholicism, such as could be found in the discipline of the Church of England, provided the best available approximation to the ultimate order within which man could find meaning and fulfilment.

III

How different is the setting and atmosphere of Lawrence's earliest days! For Eliot the large family and the comfortable circumstances in St Louis, father and mother united in the dignity of the tradition of New England culture, upholding the intellectual and moral ideals of the Unitarian Church – and over against this a miner's cottage in a Nottinghamshire village, with the possibilities of higher education for all but a tiny minority only just becoming available, and with the only centres for emotional and cultural uplift the village chapels with their sermons and hymns, their class-meetings and social entertainments.

The brilliant picture of home-life painted in *Sons and Lovers* reveals a father not wholly bad – a brave workman in the pit, a dexterous handyman at home, a nature in which there was tenderness and real affection, a physique showing elements of handsomeness and strength. But he was of violent temper, at times deceitful, constantly stumbling to excess in the public house. The mother in contrast came of refined

Puritan stock; she was well-educated, loved beauty in nature and handicrafts, wrote with style and wit, was utterly loyal to the standards of worship and ethics belonging to her Congregational chapel. Lawrence described them later:

> I was born among the working classes and brought up among them. My father was a collier, and only a collier, nothing praiseworthy about him. He wasn't even respectable, in so far as he got drunk rather frequently, never went near a chapel, and was usually rather rude to his little immediate bosses at the pit.
>
> My mother was, I suppose, superior. She came from town, and belonged really to the lower bourgeoisie. She spoke King's English, without an accent, and never in her life could even imitate a sentence of the dialect which my father spoke and which we children spoke out of doors. She wrote a fine Italian hand ... and as she grew older she read novels again.[6]

In matters of religion it was natural for him to follow his mother's example. Eliot was to dismiss this as simply 'vague hymn-singing pietism'. But Lawrence himself, in spite of the fact that in his late adolescence he turned his back upon it, never despised it as cheap or worthless. It had awakened in him the sense of wonder; it had given him a sense of rhythm; it had filled his imagination with the language and images of the Bible. 'I liked our chapel which was tall and full of light and yet still. And over the organ loft: O worship the Lord in the beauty of holiness.' In a later reflection he wrote:

> I think it was good to be brought up a Protestant; and among Protestants, a Nonconformist, and among Nonconformists a Congregationalist. Which sounds pharisaic. But I should have missed bitterly a direct knowledge of the Bible, and a direct relation to Galilee and Canaan, Moab and Kedron, those places that never existed on earth. And in the Church of England one would hardly have escaped those snobbish hierarchies of class, which spoil so much for a child. And the Primitive Methodists, when I was a boy, were always having 'revivals' and being 'saved'. I always had a horror of being saved. So, altogether, I am grateful to my 'Congregational' upbringing.[7]

Yet as he began to discover a wider world and to read its literature, he became agnostic and sceptical. He questioned the orthodox creed. Possessing a razor-like intelligence, he examined the religion of his girl friend – the religion in which she lived and moved and had her being. He discussed Renan with her. And at length, as he talked with his mother, it must have been true of him as it was of Paul Morel in *Sons and Lovers.*

> Religion was fading into the background. He had shovelled away all the beliefs that would hamper him, had cleared the ground, and come more or less to the bedrock of belief that one should feel inside oneself for right and wrong, and should have the patience to gradually realize one's God. Now *life* interested him more.[8]

For a while he attached himself to a Unitarian chapel and developed an interest in theories of social uplift. But all the time he was seeking for a religion that would satisfy the emotional drives and the aesthetic yearnings which were thrusting his soul towards some mysterious ultimate whose secret constantly tantalized and eluded him. The tragedy of his mother's suffering and death almost overwhelmed him – he knew death in its bitterest physical form. Only a religion which could bring some resolution of the almost unbearable tensions within human relationships, only a religion which could gather suffering and corruption and death within its embrace and somehow generate the promise of fresh and expanding *life*, above all, only a religion which grew out of a sense of wonder and could continually extend man's sense of wonder could win the allegiance of this 'religious, earnest, suffering man'.

Such in brief are the early backgrounds of these two men of genius. The first twenty-seven years of Eliot's life were, so far as we can judge, relatively untroubled. Some distaste, perhaps, for the uglier aspects of a mid-Western city; some dissatisfaction with the faith of his fathers and the bland religious optimism of many of their successors: some stress of mind and imagination in seeking for a unifying philosophy of life. But in the main the story is one of steady expansion of knowledge and experience; residence in new countries, in new worlds of literature, amongst new acquaintances and friends. Though a substantial interest in the place of religion in human life was maintained, there is no evidence that this led to any kind of personal conviction or commitment.

In contrast, the first twenty-six years of Lawrence's life were spent in the midst of family tensions, social frictions, emotional upheavals, drab surroundings. An unpredictable father, a devoted but utterly possessive mother, an uphill struggle to obtain education, a sensitive nature in revolt against the encroachment of black industrialism, the torture of unsatisfied sex. He was, indeed, reading voraciously but academic life, as he experienced it, seemed constrictive rather than expansive. He despised all attempts to create intellectual or moral systems. And though he was ever seeking a religion that could be recognized as universally valid and relevant, he could never find in the orthodoxies of his time anything to which he could commit himself as the expression of ultimate truth.

Yet, as early as 1911, Lawrence's first novel was published and by 1915 he had written one of the most brilliantly imaginative works of our own or indeed of any century. He was pouring himself out – ideas, images, insights, experiences, encounters – all taking shape through his mastery of the English tongue: in *The Rainbow* he already reached the heights. In contrast his immensely learned contemporary was moving with deliberate caution, with intense concentration, seeking an exact and economic form to communicate the crystallization of his thoughts and feelings. It was not until 1943 that his own masterpiece appeared: in *Four Quartets* the knowledge of human life obtained through years of disciplined study, brooding contemplation, technical experimentation and personal suffering finally gained expression in a few hundred lines of dramatic verse.

Lawrence, we feel, was a man ever expanding, even exploding, to the limits of human expression. In his *Study of Thomas Hardy*, for instance, he claimed an affinity with him in that, for both, their characters 'are always bursting suddenly out of bud and taking a wild flight into flower – it is all explosive, the self suddenly bursts the shell of manner and convention and commonplace opinion and acts independently, absurdly, without mental knowledge or acquiescence'.[9] Eliot, on the other hand, was a man ever pressing inwards towards the heart of reality, seeking stillness and reconciliation at the very 'eye' of the hurricane of life.

There are magnificent evocations of religious 'feeling' in *The Rainbow*. There is a beautiful portrayal of Will Brangmen's devotion to his parish church and of his sense of fulfilment when at peace within its atmosphere. The chapter entitled 'The Cathedral' contains the finest verbal expression that I know of the peculiar dual sensation of abasement and uplift that a great Gothic building can inspire. Lawrence himself must have felt these sensations intensely. But his search for the ultimate did not end in the great spaces of Lincoln cathedral: even here the spell was broken by Anna who found herself resisting her husband's near ecstasy. It is not through the sense of the numinous alone that the universal hunger for the real can be satisfied. On the contrary, Lawrence was convinced that somehow the ultimate mystery could only be discovered within the experience of personal related-ness. The polarity between man and woman was somehow, he be-lieved, the key to the mystery: the 'polarized connection with other beings'.

'The source of all life and knowledge', he wrote, 'is in man and women, and the source of all living is in the interchange and the meet-ing and mingling of these two; man-life and woman-life, man-knowledge and woman-knowledge, man-being and woman-being.'[10] In his poem *Cypresses* he wrote:

> Evil, what is evil?
> There is only one evil, to deny life.

And if there was one book above all others which seemed to stimulate and direct his imagination towards the desired goal, it was, strangely enough, the Book of Genesis whose language and imagery he never ceased to love.

The rainbow is his supreme symbol: it holds the promise of perfect union within a new order. Man and woman soar aloft from their re-spective bases and find their symbolic fulfilment in its perfect arch. So the sons of God become mysteriously united with the daughters of men. The old order perishes in the deluge, and the rainbow promises the new creation of the living God. Ursula Brangwen believed that the man would come out of Eternity to which she belonged. 'She saw in the rainbow the earth's new architecture, the old, brittle corruption of houses and factories swept away, the world built up in a living fabric of Truth, fitting to the over-arching heaven.'[11]

In his last substantial novel, *The Man Who Died*, Lawrence tried to portray this man coming out of eternity as a Christ who first passed through death and then became united with the archetypal feminine of earth. This particular vision may seem in many ways artificial and bizarre. Yet it symbolizes the positive truth towards which Lawrence was always struggling – the truth that only within a genuine relation-ship where there is no absorption of the one by the other, no isolation of the one from the other, but a continuous magnetic interchange between poles of identity – only within such a relationship can religion reach its highest and most authentic expression.

IV

There is no formal consistency in Lawrence's many references to religion. Sometimes he described the religious sense as a kind of sixth sense – a natural sense of wonder.

> When the wonder has gone out of a man he is dead. When all comes to all, the most precious element in life is wonder. Love is a great emotion and power is power. But both love and power are based on wonder. Plant consciousness, insect consciousness, fish consciousness, animal consciousness, all are related by one permanent element, which we may call the religious element in all life, even in a flea: the sense of wonder. That is our sixth sense. And it is the *natural* religious sense . . .
> Science in its true condition of wonder is as religious as any religion. But didactic science is as dead and boring as dogmatic religion. Both are wonderless and productive of boredom, endless boredom.[12]

At other times he emphasized the intimate association of religion with life.

> Somehow I think we come into knowledge (unconscious) of the most vital parts of the cosmos through touching things. Such a touch is the connection between the vigorous flow of two lives. Like a positive electricity, a current of creative life runs through two persons and they are instinctive with the same life-force.[13]

This reflection appeared in a letter written as early as 1908. It reveals Lawrence's insight, gained in spite of his abhorrence of all forms of industrialism, that man's knowledge of the properties of electricity can provide him with illuminating metaphors for the description of psychic structures and energies. Contact, current, poles, elements, magnetism are vivid images for the representation of that which had become basic in his experience – the meeting, the encounter, the relationship which makes the life-flow possible. For him the all-important issue was the surge of life, the ecstasy of life, the free unhindered flow of life. Religion must be concerned with the experience and celebration of the life-flow at its maximum intensity.

But no one has been more conscious than Lawrence of the great enemy of life: he was almost obsessively aware of death in all its forms. So he returned again and again to the great polarities of human experience – light and dark, sun and moon, creativity and destruction, primitivism and civilization, the conscious and the unconscious, the intellect and the blood, the spirit and the flesh, male and female. Each of these pairs may, in isolation, become an instrument of death: in creative union, in the moment of meeting, there is renewal of life.

Out of this conviction, it seems, came his quarrel with Christianity. Both in the Anglicanism and in the Nonconformity of his young manhood, the dominant intellectual movements had been inspired by a Platonic idealism which gloried in the subjection of matter to spirit, of fleshly sensation to reason and logic. Ethically, the whole emphasis had been upon love as the supreme Christian virtue, love interpreted all too often in conventional and sentimental terms without regard to the complexities of social justice and political power. The only hope for Christianity, he believed (and this may have been the prophetic burden of *The Man Who Died*) was to be re-born through men and women yielding to, being embraced by, the primitive drives and sensations which belong to real flesh and blood, to the body and the unconscious, to the dark underworld of the earth mother, to the sources of fertility and vitality. Only through magnetic polar relationship could the creation in all its fullness be renewed.

Yet the eternal, he urged, cannot be expressed in terms of any single earthly manifestation. For Lawrence, Osiris, Christ, Dionysus are of equal significance in so far as each bears witness to the triumph of life over death. He refused to be imprisoned within any exclusive religious form. All the great images of religion were for him projections of human experiences and retained their validity only to the extent that they quicken the imagination for further adventure into the realities of the kingdom of life.

But if outward and visible symbolic forms had obvious limitations for the representation of a reality which could be known only in moments of meeting, there was one literary form eminently suitable for this purpose: it was the novel.

> Philosophy, religion, science, they are all of them busy nailing things down, to get a stable equilibrium. But the novel, no. The novel is the highest example of subtle interrelatedness that man has discovered. Everything is true in its own time, place, circumstance. If you try to nail anything down, in the novel, either it kills the novel or the novel gets up and walks away with the nail.[14]

'The highest example of subtle interrelatedness', a 'tremulation on the ether', the revelation of the relation between man and his circumambient universe at the living moment – such were Lawrence's definitions of the art-form which he believed to be supremely capable of capturing the moments of meeting in which true life can alone be realized. Novel after novel came from his pen in an almost feverish haste. And when he was able to rise to what he called 'the maximum of our imagination' then the 'religious' came to momentary expression. The great Rudolf Otto found it impossible to express the experience of 'religion' except by recourse to such terms as the 'numinous' and the *mysterium tremendum et fascinans*. Lawrence attempted no such shorthand definitions. As his imagination soared, in writing about human relationships and the peak experiences of human living, the sense of some religious ultimate made itself felt. He was content to tell a story, believing that it was the superlative medium for conveying to others that sense of ultimate mystery which was the object of his constant search.

V

In Eliot's references to religion there is a far greater emphasis on form, but there is no attempt to develop a system or to give a comprehensive interpretation of the place of religion in human life. The most obvious contrast to Lawrence is in his insistence that religion is a matter of the intellect and the will, whereas for Lawrence it was intimately concerned with feeling and the blood. Eliot had little sympathy with the forms of revivalism which had stirred the emotions and numbed the intelligences of so many mid-Westerners at the end of the nineteenth century. If religion was to have any place in his philosophy of life it must be related to the totality of human experience, both in space and in time.

So far as this totality was concerned, he depended largely upon the sacred books both of the Christian faith and of other religions, upon the mythology and drama of the Graeco-Roman world, and upon the researches and reports of social anthropologists. In 'The Waste Land' he drew together these various strands and wove them into a pattern of death as the gateway to new life. In this poem death is in the foreground – death with its symbolic associates – the desert, drought, darkness, sterility. But even when death seems to be final, there is still the possibility of regeneration. The ultimate mystery of things, towards which man's sacrificial rituals in all parts of the world have been feeling, is that of the transcending of human tragedy: through death, rebirth: through the willingness to enter into the darkness, the emergence into the light of a new day.

Eliot's general recognition of and intellectual acceptance of the law of sacrifice was to receive its particular actualization and confirmation when later he committed himself to Christian faith and discipline. But that this law was part of the very structure of the universe in which we live, and that it was the chief determinant of men's religious practices, had become clear to him at a much earlier stage in his life. It was not enough to focus attention, as his Puritan and Unitarian forebears had tended to do, upon particular moral offences which could be defined and condemned and avoided. There were deeper roots of evil in the human condition, a negativity expressed by symbols of loneliness, numbness, purposelessness, meaninglessness; a futility expressed by symbols of sterility, aridity, vacuity; an impurity expressed by symbols of disease, infection, contamination. No system of external rules and punishments could deal with this deep-seated ailment. Only some form of death, actual or symbolic, could bring it to an end and in so doing make possible a new beginning.

This universal law, recognizable through the world's myths and rituals, could be seen in clearer definition in its actual historical manifestations. We are heirs to a tradition, a tradition which fastens upon particular events and particular experiences as bearing a more-than-ordinary significance. History, Eliot would ultimately affirm, is 'a pattern of timeless moments'. There are moments so fraught with meaning, so powerful in their impact upon the human consciousness, that they cannot fail to be remembered, to be celebrated, to take their place as the all-important clues to life's total significance. In these moments time seems to stand still. One stage ends, another begins. These are the profoundest experiences to which man ever bears witness, and they demand the serious attention of all who come after. Thus there is a tradition of particular human experience to which each of us in his own way falls heir. The question is how we respond to it. Rejection? Indifference? Surrender?

In Eliot's case the time came when he deliberately identified himself with the company of those who had, they believed, experienced the presence of the divine in moments when human ambition and human desire and human striving had been halted and when, as in the critical example of the one annunciation, they had been prepared to say 'Be it unto me according to thy Word'. Such an experience had never come easily: in fact it had cost not less than everything. It had involved renunciation, dispossession, self-surrender, agony, even martyrdom and death. But it followed the pattern established by the One who had become incarnate at the central, critical moment of time.

In and through his particular death and resurrection, the general pattern of universal sacrifice was focussed, clarified and confirmed.

If Lawrence was for ever seeking the secret of the flow of life and the meaning of reciprocal human relationships, Eliot was for ever seeking the secret of order and the meaning of peak experiences recorded in the human story. A recurring word in *Four Quartets* is 'pattern'. He was convinced that, in spite of all appearances to the contrary, human history was to be regarded not as mere sequence nor as simple development – certainly not as distraction and randomness with no concentration or meaning. There is a pattern. It is a pattern indeed which is new in every disclosure and yet which always involves some renunciation, some self-surrender, some descent into the darkness, in fact some form of sacrifice. And it is always marked by an experience of stillness. The very notion of bringing one condition to an end implies the further idea of turning and in the moment between the times, between two waves of the sea, we can become aware of an utter stillness in which the presence of God is supremely manifest.

Again and again Eliot employs the word 'still' (or its noun 'stillness'). 'The still point of the turning world' becomes a sacramental expression of the divine presence.

> at the still point, there the dance is,
> But neither arrest nor movement . . .
> Neither movement from nor towards,
> Neither ascent nor decline. Except for the point, the
> still point,
> There would be no dance, and there is only the
> dance.[15]

Words 'creak, strain, break, fail' – Eliot admits as much. Yet the intolerable wrestle with words must continue. On the one hand he tries to bear witness to the pattern of sacrifice which constitutes the very grain of God's universe and on the other hand he seeks to guide the imagination towards the point of stillness, darkness, intense desiccation, where, at the end of human struggling, there is the moment of revelation and the assurance that love is the ultimate reality. No medium is as suitable for the communication of this truth as the poem. A poem brings the past into the present, for its words have a history of use and meaning. It dies in the present, for once the words have been put in their place they have been brought, as it were, to their goal. Yet the miracle of words which, in sequence and sound, correspond to reality is that they go on resounding into the future: out of the seeming death of the formulated poem they rise up to share in newness of life with the living. So the poem, with all its imperfections, can bear witness to the perfect pattern and can guide the soul towards the experience of stillness in which the presence of God can be momentarily realized.

In his essay 'Poetry and Drama' Eliot reveals how closely for him art and religion are intertwined.

It is ultimately the function of art in imposing a credible order upon ordinary reality and thereby eliciting some perception of an order *in* reality to bring us to a condition of serenity, stillness and reconciliation; and then leave us, as Virgil left Dante, to proceed toward a region where that guide can avail us no further.[16]

VI

In exploring the nature of the universe, modern scientists focus attention upon two main categories or elements: structure and energy. In the realm of twentieth-century dramatic art Eliot has been an outstanding representative of the quest for order, structure, pattern: Lawrence of the drive towards energy, vitality, life-force. There is indeed energy in Eliot's work, shape in Lawrence's. But by their own confession, it was upon order and vitality that their respective sights were set.

I have referred to the famous passage in which Eliot describes the design of his plays as imposing a credible order upon ordinary reality and thereby eliciting some perception of an order in reality: I have drawn attention to the frequent recurrence of the term 'pattern' in *Four Quartets*. But it is hardly necessary to look for these detailed references to order. His masterpiece, *Four Quartets*, is a supreme example of ordered writing. The four elements, the four seasons, perhaps the four stages of human life: each quartet divided into five sections whose general form or character is the same in every case. In spite of all the tendencies of language and events to get out of control – certainly out of the control of men – Eliot is convinced that there *is* a controlling pattern and that the Divine Artist is all the time working to purify the imaginations and make perfect the wills of his creatures so that they may gradually become conformed to that image which is their true destiny.

In expounding this divine activity his two chief analogies are those of purification and illumination: man needs to be purged from self-seeking by the divine fire, to be delivered from self-enclosed ignorance by the coming of the divine light. Eliot revolts against the confident humanism which assumes that man can change his obviously unsatisfactory condition for the better by his own knowledge and his own skill. There must be humility before the revelation of transcendence as at the one annunciation: there must be submission to purification by fire as at the first Pentecost: there must be openness to illumination by the light as at the epiphany of the saviour of the world. And all these notes are woven together within the one pattern by which the universe is sustained and continuously redeemed – the pattern of sacrifice.

This pattern is movingly portrayed in the fourth section of 'East Coker' where the passion of the Redeemer is represented as 'an eternal act perpetually operative in time' (Helen Gardner) but it becomes even more significant for the interpretation of the poet's own experience at the conclusion of his poem 'Preludes'. Having first exposed his imagination to the squalor of a great city, the blackened street, the sordid routine of its life in the early evening, he suddenly changes from general description to four lines expressed autobiographically. Thus, we catch a glimpse of Eliot's own participation in the divine passion:

> I am moved by fancies that are curled
> Around these images, and cling:
> The notion of some infinitely gentle
> Infinitely suffering thing.

Through renunciation, self-humbling, sacrifice, the ordinary life of mankind is redeemed. Such is the pattern which in moments of intense illumination becomes visible to those whose eyes are open to the light. Once the pattern has been seen, the only course for man is to 'fare forward' in the way of discipline, obedience and faith.

Whereas Eliot found himself in revolt against the grasping uncultured individualism of much of American society at the turn of the century, Lawrence revolted against the soulless industrialism which had torn the countryside apart and condemned thousands of his fellow human beings to the kind of existence which he had known in a typical miner's cottage. His concern was not so much for order: he believed that law and submission to law had been accorded far too large a place in human history. Nor was he prepared to accept the Christian emphasis on love: he believed that this had all too easily led to a passive acceptance of the *status quo* and to sentimentality. His whole being cried out for life, new life, powerful life, pulsating life. Unless there could come a new access of vital energy into the body corporate, England, he believed, was doomed. And what he had already come to feel because of the tendencies towards decay and degeneration which he sensed in his own social situation, was magnified and intensified tenfold when war came – the 'Gadarene slope of the war', 'the slope of mechanical death'. Conventional morality, 'Christian' philanthropy, evolutionary liberalism, scientific mechanization were all alike guilty, in Lawrence's eyes, of promoting the accelerating rush towards disintegration and death.

He had no doubt that he was living in a time of tragic crisis for humanity at large. It was a time comparable to that of Noah when the deluge had almost exterminated the sons of men. It was an apocalyptic time when no mere cleansing or reforming would be of any avail: nothing less than a new heaven and a new earth, a revelation of a paradisial state could be the object of men's hopes. He was fascinated by the first and last books of the Bible with their vivid imagery, their stories of creation and new creation, their records of shattering events, their constant advances beyond the ordinary into unknown mysteries. He believed that the time was ripe for another apocalypse – the world's Third Age. Jewish law, Christian love, would be succeeded by the Age of the Spirit of Life – life which is universal, boundless, free.

In some respects Lawrence antedated Bultmann in his perception that the Bible (and in particular its strongly Hebraic elements as represented in Genesis and Revelation), is concerned not so much with a pattern (this is far more characteristic of Hellenism) as with dialectical interchange. The dialectic comes to its most vivid expressions in contrasts between light and darkness, between dry land and water, between spirit and flesh, above all between life and death. In fact, the earlier contrasts which I have detailed are all variations in their own way upon the central, never-ceasing struggle between life and death. Life cannot be separated from death nor death from life. Therefore in a certain sense Lawrence welcomes death, embraces death as the womb of life. What he cannot abide is stagnation, fixity, a mechanical rigidity, an imposed man-made system. Through vivid images (e.g. the stone hurled into the water which offers a perfect reflection of the moon), he seeks to destroy all complacencies, all closed systems, all seemingly established equilibria. He is seized by the apocalyptic vision of light out of darkness, the rainbow out of the deluge, incorruption out of corruption, creativity out of destruction. It was not by avoiding or repressing death that life could be fostered. Rather it was by 'polarized connection', magnetic interaction, that the 'spontaneous-creative fullness of being' could be attained.

The way that he chose, in order to promote this desired end, was the way of the novel, the dramatic story. Eliot chose the poem and the tragic drama – essentially the way of Greece. Lawrence told stories – the way of the Hebrew prophets and seers: vivid stories of human conflicts and catastrophes, of deaths and resurrections. In so doing he chose the way of greater danger. It was always possible that one side of the dialectic would either be made subservient to the other or become separated from the other: absorption or isolation, of each of which, in personal relations, Lawrence was desperately afraid. The 'religion' which he hoped to promote could easily seem to be the religion of the dark gods, of primitive sensuality, of Satanic destructiveness. Some will judge that the worship of the dark other was the only 'religious' consequence that could follow the reading of his stories. But at least it must be said that if the balance finally tipped in that direction it was because of his passionate concern to be true to the whole of human experience, to incorporate into his quest for fullness the divine and the demonic, and to maintain the dialectic of life – death whatever the temptation might be to settle for one or the other.

In the stories this dialectic is portrayed almost exclusively through the relatedness of individuals and particular through their sexuality. But Lawrence had wider issues in view, not simply those of social organization and cultural development; above all mysterious realms beyond the penetration of man's conscious mind. 'Wherever he looked,' Aldous Huxley has written, 'he saw more than a human being ought to see; saw more and therefore loved and hated more. To be with him was to find oneself transported to one of the frontiers of human consciousness.' And again: 'Lawrence's special gift was an extraordinary sensitiveness to what Wordsworth calls "unknown modes of being". He was always aware of the mystery of the world and the mystery was always for him a *numen*, divine; he could never forget, as most of us continually forget, the dark presence of the otherness that lies beyond man's conscious mind.'[17]

In his quest of the 'mystery', in his exploration of the methods by which man may enjoy union with and fulfilment in the mystery, Lawrence may have been guilty of perversion and excess. Yet few men have been more worthy to be called genius, and in few novels have the numinous and the demonic, the paradisial and the finally mysterious, gained such superlative expression.

— 6 —

Paul Tillich
&
Karl Jaspers

The exact nature of a philosopher's task is by no means obvious. Karl Jaspers, however, rejecting from an early age much that was being taught as philosophy in academic circles, passionately believed that his life-work from 1922 onwards was that of authentic philosophizing, whatever might be the current views of how it should be done. Paul Tillich, on the other hand, though fascinated by the philosophical books which he was reading even in his school days at the Gymnasium, never committed himself whole-heartedly to the study and teaching of philosophy. There was another subject, theology, which retained his allegiance. Throughout his life he tried to maintain a frontier or boundary stance between the two. Even professionally he alternated between chairs of philosophy and theology. Whereas Jaspers was deeply interested in theology but wholly dedicated to philosophy, Tillich could never commit himself completely to either of the two disciplines. Only in the dialectical interchange between the two could he find freedom and the fulfilment of his personal vocation.

Yet Jaspers would, I think, have agreed with Tillich's definition of the philosopher's task: it is to look at the whole of reality in order to discover within it the structure of reality as a whole. In point of fact no one can embrace the whole of reality. But it is possible to strive towards an apprehension of the pattern of reality as a whole rather than to spend one's time concentrating attention upon some limited area of the universe. 'Where unity of the whole becomes intellectual reality and is aware of itself as such,' Jaspers has written, 'philosophy is present'. Where any man tries to grasp and reflect within his own consciousness some pattern of the structuredness of the whole of reality, he is engaging in the essential philosophical enterprise. There remains the question, however, whether the structure itself can ever be expressed in a unified way or whether there may be elements in the total picture which demand to be interpreted by a method other than that of an integrative philosophy. Tillich believed that there were such elements and that, because of this, theology had a legitimate role to play. But even so he would never allow that philosophy and theology could operate in separate compartments. As a theologian he tried to remain a philosopher, and conversely so. Jaspers' exclusive dedication to philosophy was for him impossible.

Although the two men differed in their views of the relationship between philosophy and theology, they were united in their conviction that only one kind of philosophizing was in fact open to them in their own particular situations and circumstances. Each made himself familiar with the great philosophies of the past; each was aware that there had been periods in the world's history when men had sought to view reality as detached spectators and to make statements about it which, they claimed, were universally true. But in the period after the First World War, when the very foundations of human existence seemed to have been shaken, each found himself constrained to attempt the philosophical task in what can broadly be described as the *existentialist* way. To interpret the whole of reality existentially was their common ambition and concern. To discover how, in spite of this, they reached radically different conclusions about the nature of religious experience and Christian faith will be the object of enquiry in this chapter.

I

Karl Jaspers was born in 1883 in Oldenburg, a town in the extreme north-west of Germany, not far from the coast of the North Sea. His boyhood seems to have been singularly happy. His parents had long associations with the land, their ancestors having been farmers for many generations. Karl's father had attained a position of high responsibility in public affairs; he was also a keen painter and huntsman. The home was cultured but not religious. On the father's side reason was the final arbiter, on the mother's an unfailing love. 'Her spirit filled us with courage and determination; her wisdom gave us warmth and the assurance of security.'

However, school life in the Gymnasium proved to be far less agreeable. Here he encountered for the first time an organization which demanded unquestioning obedience to rules of a semi-militaristic character. Though outward resistance was impossible, the boy inwardly rebelled against what was utterly alien to the atmosphere in which he had been reared and the result was that he became largely estranged from the school community. While enjoying rich compensations through the supportive life of the home and through abundant opportunities to explore the beauties of the countryside, he was deprived of the easy relationships with his own contemporaries through which the ability to communicate with a wider world is created and nourished.

His interests intellectually were exceptionally broad and varied and it was not easy to decide upon a special course of study when entering university. However, after beginning with law, he made the unexpected decision in 1902 to enrol as a student of medicine and in 1909 received his Doctor's degree. In describing what lay behind this decision, Jaspers recalls the sense of loneliness which he felt during his adolescent years and the consequent urge to discover for himself some acceptable role in society.

> What should I do? Life had to find a foundation; for however marvelous specific experiences, scattering one's attention among them had a devastating effect. It became necessary to enter upon a concrete path of leading one's own life; above all my university studies now had to have a (definite) goal. I wanted to discover what knowledge is possible; medicine seemed to me to open the widest vista, having all of the natural sciences and man as its object of investigation. As a physician I could find my justification in society.[1]

A firm decision concerning his own existence, an openness to the widest possible vista: already these two factors had become crucially important in his outlook.

These characteristics of the inner world of spirit were inevitably qualified by two major influences of a more external kind. First there was a chronic sickness to which he had been subject from his earliest years but which was only diagnosed when he was eighteen years of age. It brought on bouts of fever and lassitude and could only be checked by adherence to a strict discipline of ordered habits and limited expenditures of energy. Whatever freedom he possessed was freedom within limits. Decisions had constantly to be made as to what was to be done in given circumstances if reasonable health was to be preserved. On the other hand, such questions as that of enlisting for military service in the First World War were settled beforehand: his body was simply incapable of bearing prolonged strain.

But whereas the necessity to be constantly on the watch and to husband his resources tended to accentuate his alienation from the ordinary life of society, a second influence entering his life in 1908 not only enlarged his vision of the meaning of human existence beyond anything he had previously known, but also removed many of the barriers to free communication which had hitherto caused him frustration and disappointment. This was his meeting with a remarkably gifted woman, Gertrude Mayer, member of a pious Jewish family and at that time a student of philosophy. Their mutual attraction was immediate and in 1910 they were married. In a moving description of their partnership in life Jaspers has written:

> In contrast to me, who was suffering only from my own illness, the very foundations of things had been torn asunder for her, leading to insoluble questions. [The reference is in particular to the grievous mental suffering of a sister and the tragic death of a close friend.] In her I saw the reality of a soul which refused to live by illusions. She was capable of infinite endurance in silence.
>
> In her my own affirmation of life encountered the spirit who from now on would prevent any premature acquiescence on my part. Now philosophy began, in a new way, to become a serious concern for me. We found ourselves united in its pursuit, but had not reached the goal. Thus it has remained until to-day throughout a long life together.
>
> The gloom and consciousness of constant danger induced an inescapable seriousness in her. But, out of this soil grew the infinite happiness of her immediate presence. I experienced the deep satisfaction of love which has been able to give meaning to each day even until now.[2]

Before committing himself to his final profession as a philosopher Jaspers gained invaluable practical experience of the operations of the human mind by working for seven years in the psychiatric hospital at Heidelberg. There he found a situation in which the treatment of nervous ailments was confined almost entirely to physical manipulations. Yet he came increasingly to believe that the object of psychiatry was

the whole man, his mind, his personality, his language, his relationships
with others. He set to work to write a text book on psycho-pathology,
not attempting to propagate a particular technique but, by drawing
upon his own collection of case-histories, constructing and comparing
a series of analogies derived from the natural sciences which could serve
to clarify the nature and activities of human consciousness without en-
closing it within a single dogmatic system. His constant urge was to
comprehend man as a whole.

> What mattered was to survey all possible pictures without lapsing
> into any . . . Despite the fact that, within limits, all of them [i.e. all
> existing methods of explanation] were fruitful, the supposed totality
> every time proved to be a totality within the one comprehensive
> totality of being human, never this totality itself. For the totality of
> man lies way beyond any conceivable objectifiability.[3]

To observe and reflect upon actual experience of human behaviour,
then to construct 'pictures' or 'analogies' out of materials supplied by
the natural sciences, to collate and compare these 'pictures' and as far
as possible to establish some kind of provisional order: this was Jaspers'
method of working. He was convinced that it was impossible to give a
fully comprehensive account of man and yet he was always striving
towards comprehensiveness. There are innumerable ways of enquiring
about man as he is in himself and innumerable pictures may be drawn.
But the final mystery of the individual human personality remains un-
breached. To strive for a total understanding of man, all the time knowing that such a total comprehension is impossible – this was to become
the paradoxical nature of Jaspers' life-work. From psychiatry he moved
forward into the field of wider psychological theory: from psychology
he graduated, as it were, into the all-embracing role of the philosopher.
In 1921 he was appointed to a chair of philosophy in Heidelberg, was
deprived of his professional status in 1937 but re-instated in 1945,
moved to the University of Basel in 1948 where he continued to
teach until his retirement. The philosopher ever reaching out towards
the apprehension of reality as a whole – this is an adequate summary
of his career from 1921 onwards. Like a circumnavigator of the
globe, he constantly pressed forward towards the horizon, knowing
in his heart that he could never reach finality. The goal is beyond
every horizon. Yet the philosophical quest commanded his complete
devotion from beginning to end of his academic life.

II

If Jaspers' life story can be entitled 'Towards the Horizon', Tillich's is most aptly described as 'On the Boundary'. This is in fact the title of his first autobiographical sketch prepared as a preface to the book which introduced him to many English-speaking readers: *The Interpretation of History*. In this sketch he defined no less than twelve pairs of alternatives or antinomies between whose tensions and contrasts his own career had developed. 'It has been my fate, in almost every direction, to stand between alternative possibilities of existence, to be completely at home in neither, to take no definitive stand against either.'[4] Where there are alternative possibilities, the existential quality of life becomes manifest.

In contrast to Jaspers, who was born into a family of wide culture and liberal outlook, Tillich grew up in a home in which, though the tradition of learning was honoured and vigorously sustained, a sharp division was drawn between sacred and secular studies. His father, a Lutheran pastor, was devoted to the study of theology and this initial influence of a parent who, by virtue of his office, exercised a firm authority in learning and in life, he never fully outgrew. Though his mother came from the Rhineland, and represented therefore a more liberal and democratic organization of experience than was characteristic of Eastern Germany, her early death deprived the boy of the full benefit of what she might have contributed to his development.

The very structure of the small town in Eastern Germany where Tillich lived between the ages of four and fourteen (he was born in 1886)[5] emphasized the authority of the religious tradition which governed virtually every aspect of the life of the community. 'The town was mediaeval in character. Surrounded by a wall, built around an old Gothic church, entered through gates with towers over them, administered from a mediaeval town hall, it gave the impression of a small, protected and self-contained world.' And in this world his father occupied a position of immense responsibility. Not only was he pastor of the church at Schönfliess, he was also superintendent of a group of surrounding parishes. Even the educational system was dominated by its affiliation with the church.

It would not have been surprising if a boy, living in a strictly governed pastor's home, educated in a Confessional Lutheran school, and worshipping regularly in a church with its long tradition of Lutheran piety, had either identified himself fully with the existing system or reacted against its narrow limitations and abandoned its doctrine and discipline for ever. In fact the young Tillich did neither. Instead, as he has so vividly recalled, he finally moved out from the certainties and securities of Lutheran conservatism without ceasing to treasure the positive values of the Christian tradition: he moved into the most advanced circles of cultural activities and philosophical debates without ceasing to be aware of their inadequacy and even meaninglessness if they failed to pay attention to those 'ultimate concerns' from which no life which is truly human is exempt.

Life within a pastor's home at the end of the nineteenth century may have had its restrictions but it also had its compensations. There were books, not only theological but also philosophical. There was the annual vacation which took the Tillich family to the shores of the Baltic Sea. There were journeys to the metropolis on church business, which Paul was allowed to share with his father, thereby gaining an initiation into the exciting life of Berlin around the turn of the century. It was through these varying experiences that the growing boy became familiar with wider worlds of knowledge and feeling than were to be found in the Bible and the institutional life of the church. He found increasing delight in the wonders and mysteries of the natural order – forest and corn-fields, clouds and sunset. Above all the sea stirred the very depths of his being. On vacation he would build a tall sandcastle, perch himself on top of it and stay for long periods contemplating the depth, the abyss, the meeting of finite and infinite, and sometimes the dynamic, exhilarating, almost ecstatic surging of the waves. Of all the symbolic forms that became so important a feature of Tillich's theology, it is doubtful if any exercised so abiding and so powerful an influence upon his own imagination as water in general and the sea in particular.

In retrospect, Tillich declared that it was through the actual process of philosophical debate that he was able to make the most decisive break with his father's conservative Lutheran outlook, an outlook which governed his activities, not only in the context of the church but also in that of the state and nation. Within the Lutheran tradition philosophy was accorded a place of legitimacy, even of honour.

In the tradition of classical orthodoxy, my father loved and used philosophy, convinced that there can be no conflict between a true philosophy and revealed truth. The long philosophical discussions which developed belong to the most happy instances of a positive relation to my father. Nevertheless, in these discussions the break-through occurred. From an independent philosophical position a state of independence spread out into all directions, theoretically first, practically later. It is this difficult and painful break-through to autonomy which has made me immune against any system of thought or life which demands the surrender of this autonomy.[6]

'The break-through' was effected, as Tillich himself explains, by appealing to the 'Protestant principle': this criticizes the very system of Protestant orthodoxy which had come into being as the aftermath of the exercise of that principle at the time of the Reformation. His father gloried in the heritage of Protestantism of which he regarded himself an authoritative exponent and defender. The son declared that the very principle which had made this Protestantism possible was of perennial relevance as critic and destroyer of any and every system which claimed absolute authority for itself.

The Protestant principle, in name derived from the protest of the 'protestants' against decisions of the Catholic majority, contains the divine and human protest against any absolute claim made for a relative reality, even if this claim is made by a Protestant church. The Protestant principle is the judge of every religious and cultural reality, including the religion and culture which calls itself 'Protestant'.[7]

The importance of the 'Protestant principle' in the whole of Tillich's career can hardly be exaggerated. It was this which set him free from his father's intellectual domination and gave him a sense of 'autonomy'. Yet he knew that this autonomy must never be absolutized; his own life and thought were to be constantly subjected to criticism by the same principle that had given him his initial freedom. And this was equally true of all systems, whether of theology or philosophy, of art or of science. To accept wholeheartedly the validity of the Protestant principle meant inevitably a 'boundary' type existence. No final security could ever be found in this world. Yet however painful the tension might at times prove to be, Tillich accepted his destiny with courage and conviction: he would live between theology and philo-sophy, between church and society, between religion and culture, between theory and practice, between the Lutheran doctrine of the kingdom of God and socialist idealism, between home and alien land.

His professional career between 1912, when he was ordained in the Evangelical Lutheran Church, to the time when he was forced to leave

Germany in 1933, was divided almost equally between the teaching of philosophy and of theology, in both of which disciplines he had, in students days, gained high qualifications. But his activities were not confined to teaching. In the First World War he served as chaplain in the German army from 1914 to 1918 and his experiences in the trenches clearly exercised a decisive influence upon his whole understanding of reality. He never wrote about it in detail but near the end of his life spoke of 'one moment in the war, in the middle of a terrible battle, which I would always call a *kairos* in my own life'.[8] This was in July 1916, during the battle of Champagne, when 'he witnessed the suffering and death of hundreds of casualties in the division in which he served as chaplain. The horror of that night, during which he lost some of his friends, never left him, and the whole structure of classical idealism under which the war had taken place was shattered.'[9]

Close contact on the battlefield with men from all classes awoke in Tillich a deep concern for social justice. With the defeat of Germany and the collapse of most of its traditional structures, the way seemed open for real advance towards a Christian ordering of society. He threw his energies into active support of the 'religious socialism' movement, believing that the crisis in Germany's very existence could well be one of the *kairoi* with which history itself seemed to be punctuated, an opportunity for new life to spring out of the jaws of defeat and death. Although his hopes for wide acceptance of a truly religious socialism were sadly disappointed, Tillich never ceased to relate himself theologically, wherever opportunity occurred, to the revolutionary movements in society which grew in strength the world over from the 1920s onwards.

One other decisive influence in Tillich's personal development must be mentioned. It was his exposure to great works of art and in particular to the paintings of the masters. In school days his imagination was gripped by the Greek tragedians and by Shakespeare. Hamlet captivated him and 'To be or not to be' became the quintessential summary of his own condition. But it was the discovery of painting that had an overwhelming effect upon his interpretation of reality.

It happened during the four years of war, as a reaction from the gruesomeness, the ugliness, and destructiveness of war. From my pleasure in the poor reproductions that were obtainable at the military bookstores in the fields there grew a systematic study of the history of art. From this study came the experience of art, chief of all that first experience, like a revelation, of a picture by Botticelli, when I went to Berlin on my last furlough of the War. Upon experience followed reflection and philosophic and theologic interpretation, which led me to the fundamental categories of my philosophy of religion.[10]

This interest in art was deepened and extended soon after the war through his marriage to one who was herself a painter and a lover of poetry. Together they travelled to Italy where the treasures of early Christian art made an indelible impression upon his imagination. What no amount of study of church history had brought was accomplished by the mosaics in ancient Roman basilicas. Henceforward he was to find himself standing again and again on the frontier between religion and art, between theology and art criticism. From the experience of art he derived theories, images, categories for his interpretation of religion: from the tradition and experience of religion he derived principles for the criticism and interpretation of art. To distinguish between the experience of religion and the experience of great art would never be easy. Yet he was convinced that there was a distinction. It had to be re-affirmed again and again in the moment when, in the presence of some great work of art, he felt himself grasped by an ultimate concern.

III

In many respects the life stories of these two men between the mid 1880s and the year 1920 were utterly dissimilar. Yet each fell in love with philosophy and each ultimately determined to do philosophy existentially. What does this mean?

It is significant that Jaspers deliberately turned from the study of law (a subject largely concerned with abstractions, general rules, fine verbal distinctions) to the study of medicine (a subject whose whole concentration is upon man himself, man in his concreteness, man in his bodily and mental functions). Having first acquired the basic knowledge and skills needed for his regular accreditation, he went on to specialize in the realm of the mind or psyche: at a time when psychology was only in its infancy as an academic subject, Jaspers contracted to write his text-book on psycho-pathology and soon afterwards undertook the more daring enterprise of examining the psychological motivations and attitudes associated with total views of the universe. Through all these years he was acquainting himself with case-histories revealing modes of human behaviour. By the time that war broke out in 1914 he had accumulated an impressive store of experience which enabled him to speak with authority on man, his constitution, his behaviour-patterns, his relationships, his anxieties, his breakdowns, his aspirations.

Jaspers had become convinced that it was impossible to give a comprehensive interpretation of man in terms simply of bodily and mental processes, of empirically observed behaviour and of a rationally constructed framework of measurement. And what had become his conviction in the course of semi-private practice was re-inforced in an unmistakable way by the events taking place on the stage of world history. What could be said about the depths of man's own being in the light of the stresses and strains, the heroisms and the follies of a war in which Europe was tearing itself to pieces? 'Unforgettable those years in which – under the pressure of the first world war, in the midst of hardships which we, at that time, shared with all other citizens – I found with my wife the happiness of thinking in this manner [i.e. about one's own being], in which we philosophized and, more clearly than before, found the way to ourselves.'[11]

A further re-inforcement of this way of thinking came through his discovery of the works of Kierkegaard in 1914. Until then these works, though not unknown, had made little impact upon continental philosophers. But to Jaspers they brought a major illumination, especially through their central concern for existential thinking. In passionate and defiant opposition to the way of doing philosophy which had established itself in European academic circles from the middle of the seventeenth century – logical, rational, scientific, systematic, objective, idealistic – Kierkegaard cried out that all such thinking could issue in nothing more than grandiose theoretical schemes remote from and irrelevant to human existence in its depth and intensity. Kierkegaard's cry struck an immediate resounding chord in Jaspers' inner being. Without in the least renouncing the necessity for clear and rational thought to bring order into life's experiences, he regarded as more important still the need to focus attention upon the whole man, to be concerned with the thinker himself, to observe him in his efforts to communicate with his fellows, to identify with him as he grappled with the ultimate situations of human existence, to enter into his struggles towards transcendence, to discover in what sense he is free to become himself or to advance beyond himself. *Existenz* became a key-word for Jaspers. To philosophize existentially was, from 1916 onwards, the ruling passion of his life.

In Tillich's case the commitment to an existentialist approach to reality occurred in a somewhat different way. In his autobiographical reflections he recalls his early delight in the beauties of nature and how this emotional outreach gained intellectual expression through his discovery of the writings of the romantic philosopher Schelling. These writings he read through several times and discovered in them themes for his graduate research. But Schelling, though following the general course of German idealism in his earlier works, ultimately raised serious questions about the possibility of portraying reality as a whole through any system of human categories. 'He recognized that reality is not only the appearance of essence, but also the contradiction of it and that above all human existence is the expression of contradiction to its essence; furthermore, that our thinking is part of our existence and shares the fate that human existence contradicts its true nature.'[12]

It was this seminal idea, it appears, which was decisive in influencing Tillich towards an existential approach to reality. He did not deny that there was a certain correspondence between the human spirit and reality, between what may broadly be called the subjective and the objective. But he rejected the notion that it was possible for the human mind to construct a complete system of correspondences or even a set of forms approximating to completeness. For besides correspondence there is contradiction; both in the world of appearances and in the human spirit itself. This means that all human thinking about ultimate reality must be existential. Man may be able to reach firm conclusions about the operations of the natural order to which he belongs, though even in the realm of the sciences the personal equation is by no means unimportant. But when questions are asked about being itself, about man and his relation to ultimate reality, about man and his relations with his fellow men, there is no hope of gaining answers which can be expressed in human categories systematically and finally. Man himself is deeply involved in the questions and his own existence is separated from his essence. Hence he can only speak out of his own existential situation, can only speak dialectically, for in every Yes a No lies hidden and vice versa.

These convictions, which began to form in Tillich's mind through his reading of poetry and drama and his immersion in Schelling's philosophy, were finally confirmed through his experiences in the First World War, and his deeper acquaintance after the war with the works of Kierkegaard.

The World War in my own experience was the catastrophe of idealistic thinking in general. Even Schelling's philosophy was drawn into this catastrophe. The chasm, which without doubt Schelling had seen, but soon had covered up again, opened itself. The experience of the four years of war tore this chasm open for me and for my entire generation to such an extent that it was impossible ever to cover it up. If a reunion of theology and philosophy should again become possible, it could be achieved only in such a way as would do justice to this experience of the abyss of our existence.[13]

In point of fact the 'reunion', so far as Tillich himself was concerned, could never be described as a total reconciliation or synthesis. The abyss or chasm could never finally be bridged. Only through a sustained dialectical movement could the two sides be connected and correlated.

The second confirmation of the call to think existentially had come from the voice of the solitary Danish thinker whose writings had received little attention while idealism and liberalism reigned supreme. But now, in a world shattered by war, Kierkegaard suddenly came into his own. He had in his own day faced the collapse of life's hopes and the despair of his own individual existence. Yet he had clung passionately to this extreme situation, claiming that it was in the very moment of final despair that faith and truth became real. Only at the point of the final contradiction of human confidence could the encounter with the divine become a reality.

Through his identification with figures in literature (e.g. Hamlet), through his reading of Schelling and Kierkegaard, through his overwhelming experiences in the First World War, Tillich committed himself irrevocably to the existential way of thinking. Perhaps the best expansion of what this meant to him personally is to be found in an essay on 'Philosophy and Theology' in *The Protestant Era*.

Existential is what characterizes our real existence in all its concreteness, in all its accidental elements, in its freedom and responsibility, in its failure, and in its separation from its true and essential being. Theology thinks on the basis of this existential situation and in continuous relation to it. Asking for the meaning of being, theology asks for the ultimate ground and power and norm and aim of being, as far as it is *my* being, and carries *me* as the abyss and ground of *my* existence, it asks for the threatening and promising power over *my* existence, for the demanding and judging norm of *my* existence, for the fulfilling and rejecting aim of *my* existence. In other words: In asking for the meaning of being, theology asks for God . . . It asks for the way in which man receives or resists the appearance of his ultimate concern. It asks for the way in which nature reveals or hides what concerns us ultimately. It asks for the relation of what concerns us historically to what concerns us ultimately. In other words it asks for the divine and demonic powers in ourselves, in our world, in nature as well as in history. This is existential thinking.[14]

Jaspers, then, became an existentialist philosopher by way of psychopathology, the writings of Kierkegaard and the utter disillusionment brought about by the spectacle of a World War; Tillich by way of aesthetic experience, actual involvement in war and again the writings of Kierkegaard. In course of time Tillich became well-acquainted with the works of the depth-psychologists, Jaspers with some of the great figures in the history of Western art. Thus they had much in common. Yet in matters of religion they seemed poles apart.

IV

Contemporaries from very different early backgrounds yet united in their love of philosophy and in their commitment to an existentialist approach to life: what was all this to mean when each attempted to deal with the phenomenon of religion and to define the place of religion in his total interpretation of life?

Interestingly enough, each takes pains to emphasize the ambiguity which is involved in using the word 'religion'. Jaspers wants to interpret 'religion' primarily as that attitude and activity which is hardly distinguishable from philosophy itself: the relation to transcendence, 'meditation to the very border of prayer'. In addition, however, he recognizes that 'religion' is commonly used to denote

. . . revelation as an event in the world by which God speaks directly and thereby bestows upon texts and institutions (churches) absolute authority through holiness, which demands obedience even where understanding is wanting. This religion is implied in the cult, in the actuality of something specifically holy in places, objects, acts. Finally, religion is belief in the connections of the mediation of grace by means of the authoritarian faith itself. The biggest example is the knowledge gained by grace, of one's own completed unabrogatable sinfulness, together with grace's offer of salvation by faith in the substitutionary sacrifice of God: the faith in justification by such faith.[15]

For the sake of clarity he goes on to distinguish between 'the universal concept of religion' and 'the concept of a specific religion'. With the former he is deeply concerned in all his philosophical work. With the latter he feels a kind of polar relationship. He cannot commit himself to it but at the same time he cannot ignore it. In all his philosophizing, religion in this sense remains 'like a pole which constantly concerns it, or like a weight which it cannot lift, or like an opposition which is insuperable and whose conquest, once it seems accomplished, instead of leading to the satisfaction in the now fully achieved truth, produces rather something like terror over the suddenly noticeable emptiness'. This is a remarkable statement. He philosophizes religiously by seeking to understand and express his relation to transcendence: he cannot identify himself with any specific religious cult or system of belief: yet if religion in the latter sense is excluded he feels something approaching terror because of the vacuum which has been created and which nothing else seems able to fill.

Tillich is equally insistent that there are wider and narrower concepts of religion. Indeed, he regards this distinction as fundamental in his total interpretation of life. In the seminar which took place in the spring of 1963 at the University of California, Santa Barbara, he attempted to clarify the meaning of the word 'religion' at the very outset.

If religion is defined as a state of 'being grasped by an ultimate concern' – which is also my definition of faith – then we must distinguish this as a universal or large concept from our usual smaller concept of religion which supposes an organized group with its clergy, scriptures, and dogma, by which a set of symbols for the ultimate concern is accepted and cultivated in life and thought. This is religion in the narrower sense of the word, while religion defined *as* 'ultimate concern' is religion in the larger sense of the word. The distinction of the larger concept provides us with a criterion by which to judge the concrete religions included under the smaller traditional concept. Specific religions are inherently susceptible to criticism which keeps them alive or condemns them to come to an end, if they cannot qualify under the power of this ultimate principle.[16]

Here already the contrast between the two men is clear. Jaspers, with no early background of 'specific' or cultic or dogmatic religion, feels constrained to stretch out towards transcendence in an attitude closely akin to, if not identical with, prayer and meditation: at the same time, while unable to commit himself in any way to a formal system of religion, he feels a strange sense of emptiness if his world is deprived of every manifestation of religion of this kind. Tillich, with an early background of enclosure and absorption within a traditional, dogmatic form of religion, gains his freedom through an acceptance of a larger, a universal concept of religion as 'ultimate concern': at the same time he is never willing to abandon all former religious commitments and activities but to remain within a 'narrower' system so long as it is prepared to function under the never ceasing judgment of what he sometimes called the 'Protestant principle', sometimes the criterion of 'ultimate concern'. He recognized the necessity for narrower forms of religion but fought against their claims to absolutism: Jaspers recognized the power of specific religious systems to beautify and sanctify human life (perhaps a supreme example had been provided by the circle of Jewish piety in which his wife had grown to maturity) but shrank from embracing such a system for himself, seeing that his life from its earliest beginnings had been dedicated to openness, freedom, reasonableness, the quest of the whole man. Each would have described the other as a deeply 'religious' man: the difference came when a decision had to be made about making or retaining a commitment to a particular symbolic system.

V

I have referred briefly to the definitions and general interpretations of religion which are to be found in the works of these two philosophers. These cannot however be divorced from their actual experiences, and it will be instructive to examine what they tell us of their relation to religion as cult and faith in their earliest years.

Jaspers writes frankly about his childhood. Though reckoned to be formal members of the Lutheran Church, his parents ignored the ecclesiastical world. At school he was exposed to religious instruction but it made little impression on him. Confirmation was a joke and in his last year at the Gymnasium he seriously contemplated severing all connections with the church. His father, however, urged him to postpone making so radical a decision, though he himself at the age of seventy actually left the church. The whole family atmosphere was one of freedom, independence, openness; Jaspers' father recognized the value of religion as a regulative force in society but regarded reason and love as virtues to be coveted above all that the church might demand as the necessary expressions of the religious life.

> No one taught me to pray. But my parents reared us strictly in reverence of the leading ideas of truthfulness and fidelity, in constantly meaningful activity, in free turning to the magnificence of nature and to the contents of spiritual creations. They allowed us to grow up in a full world.[17]

The time came when Jaspers, in pursuit of his philosophical quest, learned to appreciate the place that religion had played in the historical experience of mankind. Yet he himself owed little to any particular ecclesiastical tradition and had no desire to promote the cause of any particular church. On the other hand he was convinced that his own quest was in the deepest sense religious in that it was directed towards ultimate reality, towards 'universally valid facts'. Moreover his own philosophizing which, he always insisted, he carried out as an individual in his own reality (i.e. existentially) seemed in the last resort indistinguishable from the exercise of faith which is the heart of true religion.

Jaspers himself gladly admitted how greatly, in this movement towards what the Bible speaks of as 'faith', he had been helped and influenced by his wife. In a revealing passage he writes:

> A mighty impulse to the question concerning faith came to me from my wife. Quite early, and without any actual break and in substantial fidelity to her heritage, she had transformed the orthodox Jewish faith in herself into Biblically grounded philosophizing. Her life was permeated by religious reverence. Wherever she met with the religious she had respect. Since Gertrude has come to us, my father said once, Christmas becomes each year more Christian. This life without dogma and without law, from childhood on touched by the breath of the Jewish prophets, was guided by an unshakable moral unconditionality. I felt myself wondrously related to her and became encouraged to bring into the focus of consciousness what, under the veil of the intellect had been, it is true, effective but hidden.[18]

In the case of Jaspers, then, we see a life begun in an atmosphere of freedom, openness and love but with no formal 'religious' associations: continuing in an intensive study of man – his bodily functions, strengths and weaknesses, his mental processes and derangements, his strivings towards wholeness and fulfilment: strengthened and expanded by his union with a woman of reverence and faith: dedicated to the quest for truth through philosophizing which, though it honoured the great tradition of philosophical learning, struggled always to become individual, free, existential, bearing the nature and quality of religious faith. Though he never identified himself formally with any ecclesiastical institution, Jaspers became a deeply religious man if the term 'religious' is used to describe a reverence for truth and a faith in that reality which encompasses human existence yet transcends any logical or artistic representation.

It is immediately obvious how different was Tillich's early experience. From the beginning his was a boundary-type existence. On the one side the dominating authority of a father who was himself the official representative of an authoritarian ecclesiastical system: on the other side a mother who had grown up in an atmosphere 'characterized by zest of living, sensuous concreteness, mobility, rationality and democracy'.[19] But his mother's early death meant that it was the authoritarian influence which for a long time prevailed.

When he was six years old he entered the local public school

> ... which was a confessional school, completely Lutheran ... And there we had classes in religion for at least four hours a week. I learned the catechism; I learned the biblical stories; I learned the hymns. And I was a person for whom these symbols were more than adequate. They were received avidly by my subconscious and even by my consciousness and they remained there. They have been alive there ever since.[20]

And what he learned through verbal forms in school was deepened by worship in the beautiful church of which his father was pastor. The experience of the 'holy' which he received at that time became for him, he claimed, an indestructible good and 'the foundations of all my religious and theological work'.[21]

Yet these formative years were not devoid of tension. In the closed circle of home and church and school a strong, confessional, religious influence: in the wider world of nature and art a sense of mystery, of beauty and holiness beyond all human cognition or representation. And so, as his vivid autobiographical reflections reveal, the boundary remained the symbol of successive stages of his journey through life. It was not a question of a complete emancipation from the institutional and traditional aspects of religion. Rather it was the struggle to hold on to them and yet to go beyond them; to preserve the rich heritage of symbolic forms through which a constantly renewed experience of the 'holy' had been brought into human life and yet to transcend them when, in some moment of crisis, a new revelation of God was in some way disclosed.

The theological witness to the gracious activity of God in accepting the sinner and the doubter was too much a part of Tillich's own tradition and experience ever to be discounted or rejected: yet his love of philosophy drove him on to ever new discoveries in the worlds of nature and history and art. Like Jaspers he went on philosophizing existentially. But for Jaspers the supreme moments of human existence were those in which a philosophic faith stretched out or leapt out to affirm the nature of ultimate being as the 'encompassing' (a key word in his philosophy). The 'encompassing' cannot be analysed or defined. But the feel of the term is unmistakable. It seems to imply that 'all shall be well' and that 'all manner of things shall be well'. This is the ultimate reality within which faith in truth and goodness becomes possible. For Tillich on the other hand the supreme moments were those in which he was grasped, as he believed, by 'ultimate concern' (a key term in his whole philosophy). Alternatively, he spoke of that which is unconditionally important. In no sense could either of these terms refer to anything finite. Yet the infinite and ultimate shines through finite and proximate embodiments. And when through such embodiments man is grasped by the ultimate he must respond with Yes or No. It is through the Yes of faith that man can affirm the meaning of his own existence.

VI

In the last resort the difference between these two contemporaries finds its focus in their respective attitudes to revelation and particularity. A description of the meaning of revelation stands at the very forefront of Tillich's system. Only because of revelation can there be any theology at all. On the other hand Jaspers cannot even entertain the idea of revelation, except in the most open and indirect way. All appearances are in a sense given to us and we try to make sense of them. Certain ultimate situations – death, struggle, suffering, chance, guilt – challenge us, awaken us, expose our vulnerability in critical fashion but it would be inappropriate in his view to speak of them as vehicles of revelation.

Jaspers readily allows that in the course of history certain individuals claim to have received a direct revelation from God. This claim must be respected and is worthy of examination by the philosopher. But the great danger arises that the claim will be made absolute. If, because of their own certitude, the recipients proceed to force what they believe to be revealed truth upon the consciousness of others, freedom is destroyed. And it is freedom that Jaspers is always jealous to preserve but which he feels is always threatened by a doctrine of direct revelation. When one of his critics urged that there have been notable occasions when new thoughts have entered the world and become part of spiritual reality he agreed wholeheartedly. 'But', he then declared, 'to attempt to identify the revelation of God: – that he himself makes a singular appearance in time and speaks at a definite place – with that universal secret of history, this would, after all, be all too harmless a liberation from the seriousness of the assertion and attestation of the believers in revelation.'[22] 'God', he affirms in a striking statement, 'does not speak at some privileged place in space or time but rather, in so far as possible, everywhere, yet always indirectly and ambiguously. For God is hidden and every certainty about him is fraught with danger.'[23]

Jaspers' fear of any kind of authoritarian regime or of any demand which is not open to rational discussion – a fear which brought about a crisis even in school-days – stayed with him throughout his life. A particular place, a particular time, a particular person, a particular language – all these seemed to threaten his passion for openness and freedom. The 'encompassing' is that which is beyond all encompassings. It is attested, indeed, by appearances, 'ciphers', human communications, indirect language. But ultimately there is hiddenness, darkness. Man can experience an ever-expanding freedom in wonder as he soars into the unknown, an unknown which he thereby affirms to be trustworthy and the ultimate secret of his own existence.

It is abundantly clear that Tillich, in contrast, had no such fear of the particularity of revelation. Bondage, restriction, heteronomy had from the beginning been particularized in his own experience in the person of his father and in the circumstances of his Lutheran home situation. How could he attain freedom when any challenge to the care by which he was surrounded must involve him in a sense of guilt? Moreover, at the very heart of the tradition to which he belonged there was the witness to a particular person, related to a particular time and place, who had overcome the negativities and contradictions of human existence in the power of the New Being of which he was the embodiment. Though Tillich might rebel against human authority and thereby incur guilt, the revelation in Christ brought an assurance of acceptance in the realm of ultimate authority and deliverance from all the anxieties of his human existence into the spiritual liberty of the children of God. In a real sense he overcame a general bondage and fear by appealing to the particular. Henceforward his task would be to expound the relation of the particular to the general problems of human existence. Through the particular he had gained his own freedom. He would never allow it to become an instrument for the enforcement of bondage.

Nowhere in his published work, I think, does Tillich deal more forthrightly with the problem of particularity than in the seminar discussions at Santa Barbara to which I have already referred. His audience pressed him on the point but he was convinced that the symbol of Christ crucified was unique in the world's history and adequate as a criterion of judgment for every aspect of human experience. If Jaspers' basic fear was of intolerance born of belief in an exclusive revelation, Tillich's fear was of idolatry or demonization born of belief in the absoluteness of a finite embodiment of power. The radical negation of all idolatries – political, cultural and religious – was for him once for all symbolized in the spectacle of Messiah crucified.

In further elaboration of the significance of this symbol Tillich laid special emphasis on two points. First he insisted that in the biblical picture of the Christ we see no evidence of 'scars' nor of separation from God nor of interruption of continuous communion with God. He is therefore rightly acclaimed as the Christ.

I see in the image of the Christ in the New Testament a revelatory and a critical power, which may have been approached elsewhere, but which always remains the ultimate criterion. For this reason I have called Jesus as the Christ the center of history. I mean that here, at one decisive point, the relationship between God and finite man was not interrupted.[24]

This was Tillich's first emphasis which he had already affirmed in his book *Christianity and the Encounter of the World Religions*.[25] But then came the second, and in some respects the more distinctive, mark of particularity. The Christ allowed himself to be crucified. 'What is particular in him is that he crucified the particular in himself for the sake of the universal.' He sacrificed his finitude totally.

In Christianity, in the symbol of the cross, there is the fundamental revelation that he who was supposed to bring the new aeon, the new reality, the new being . . . had to sacrifice himself, in his individual character, as a bearer of the ultimate. I have expressed this idea in paradoxical terms which have often been misunderstood but to which I nonetheless adhere: Jesus sacrificed himself as Jesus to himself as the Christ. It is by this intricate form that I believe we have to interpret the symbol of the cross. Now the consequence of this concept is that Christianity, in principle, can never accept one of its actualized forms as the final form. And whenever it does so, it deviates from the fundamental understanding of the cross.[26]

Both Jaspers and Tillich regard themselves as existentialists. For both freedom is the very breath of life and freedom has to be actualized again and again. But whereas Jaspers finds the safeguard of freedom in a refusal to focus attention upon or to be committed in allegiance to any one particular symbol (all symbols are to be regarded as 'ciphers' open to an unlimited variety of interpretation), Tillich finds his safeguard in the recognition of a unique symbol possessing the power to judge, and if necessary negate, all finite forms which compete for man's ultimate commitment and obedience. For Jaspers, a unique particular would spell death to the universal: for Tillich, it is through a unique particular, in its radical negation, that universal freedom becomes possible. For Jaspers a particular revelation is a denial of man's freedom to soar towards the all-encompassing: for Tillich it is only through the judging-saving power of the cross that man is set free from all false absolutes, from subjection to all counterfeit symbols which claim to be bearers of a final authority. Jaspers was for ever seeking freedom through self-transcendence: in communication with his fellow human beings, in communication with the great figures of history, in communication with the all-encompassing other. Tillich was for ever seeking freedom through the conquest of the negative, through deliverance from estrangement, through reconciliation with the unconditioned other.[27] Here are two concepts of human freedom: fulfilment and reconciliation. May it not be that each, in its own formulation, is a valid interpretation of man's highest good?

⟿ 7 ⟿

The Word and the Spirit

I have tried to draw an outline sketch of the careers and the contributions to literature of five pairs of twentieth-century writers, all born within the span of one decade of the nineteenth. Each successive comparison has revealed both similarities and contrasts. What light do they shed upon the major distinction between general religious experience and particular Christian commitment which has become one of the leading issues of our day?

I

A *centripetal* interpretation represented by one group of writers – Dodd, Raven, Muir, Eliot, Tillich – focusses attention upon a particular place or a particular time, a particular event or a particular symbol. A *centrifugal* interpretation represented by the other group – Toynbee, Huxley, Stevens, Lawrence, Jaspers – can never allow itself to be tied to a particular place, time or happening: its concern is with openness, expansiveness, even explosion. I shall try to illustrate this tentative distinction by reference to their writings.

There can be no doubt that the first eighteen years of Dodd's life in Wrexham gave him an abiding framework of reference to which he remained loyal and for which he continued to be grateful throughout his career. Home and school and chapel together constituted an extraordinarily stable foundation. He was aware of constant encouragement from members of the 'supportive community' of which he was a part. In his nineteenth year he entered university but as soon as vacations came he was back in the familiar town, taking his place in the chapel choir and renewing his strength, like Antaeus, from the environment which had nurtured him. He was not fettered by it but he had no wish to break loose from it. *There and Back Again*, the title of the one book which he wrote for children, expresses his own adventure into the wider world with the constant return, at least in imagination, to the place where his own conception of God and his redeeming purpose for mankind had first taken shape.

While still a child Raven became fascinated by the varieties of natural life in the parks near his home. But when summer came and he reached the low-lying estuary of the Dee, with its birds and plants and fish and butterflies, with its opportunities to observe and capture and explore, he was for the time being in paradise.

It was a place throbbing with the manifestations of life. And although other places – Norfolk for example – 'A paradise where Quail and Bustards, Swallowtails and Purple Emperors took the place of the angels and elves for which, being a prosaic child, I had never had much regard'[1] later evoked a similar affection and devotion, the prototype of his Eden, the fount of organic life, had once for all been established on the flats at Parkgate.

The same is true of Edwin Muir. The place of his early idyllic years remained his Eden to the end of his life. This was not just romanticism or nostalgia. His roots were in the soil, the society, animal and human, the unbroken cycle of the natural order, associated with his island home. There the blank fields, the lumbering horses and the lonely trees seemed to be mysterious presences surrounding him and the rituals of the slaughter-house and stock-yard imprinted themselves indelibly on the child's memory. But, though awesome, these experiences were all contained within the overall security and serenity of the island home. This place of innocence was a place of a real, divine presence. Though later experience would bring 'blessings in Eden never known', still the one place, experienced, obscured, recovered, transfigured, ever re-mained an essential part of Muir's total interpretation of ordinary human existence.

In the case of Eliot, attachment to a particular place is strikingly revealed in the third of the *Four Quartets*. In boyhood days the great event of the year was the departure from the city and the re-discovery of the holiday heaven. On the rocky shore north of Boston he listened and explored until the sense of this particular place became part of his innermost being. Though the garden of Burnt Norton and the chapel of Little Gidding were to assume special significance in his later interpretation of reality, nothing attained quite the richness of personal memories and the wealth of symbolic forms associated with 'The Dry Salvages'. It was perhaps around Cape Ann that he began vaguely to sense the possibility of 'a further union, a deeper communion': the wave cry, the wind cry, the vast waters of the petrel and the porpoise, were for ever linked with the security of his summer home amidst the immovable rocks.

But the fisher-folk of Gloucester also experienced tragedy through shipwreck. And the sense of place took on special significance for Eliot when it came to be associated with martyrdom. Some years after the completion of *Four Quartets* he made a comment to a friend on these lines from 'Little Gidding':

> You are here to kneel
> Where prayer has been valid.

'What I mean', he said 'is that for some of us, a sense of place is compelling. If it is a religious place, a place made special by the sacrifice of a martyrdom, then it retains an aura. We know that once before a man gave of himself *here* and was accepted *here* and it was so important that the occasion continues to invest the place with its holiness. Of course, I am aware that not all persons have a sense of place, nor is it necessary for it to exist to make prayer valid.'[2] It was in fact unnecessary to go in search of Golgotha, a site which could never be exactly located. It was enough to know that on the steps inside Canterbury cathedral a man gave up his life, following the pattern of the One who made the supreme sacrifice for the sake of all mankind.

A place could be of the utmost significance in helping to establish that order which Eliot regarded as fundamental within any true conception of art. It is interesting that he once referred to the 'centrifugal impulse of heresies'. His own impulse was towards a centre, the still centre, the place towards which the pathways of speech converged but where speech was no longer appropriate or necessary: it was holy ground.

In Tillich's autobiographical reflections it is not exactly one place to which his memories and longings return but rather one type of place. Even so this type first powerfully influenced his imagination while he was enjoying periods of vacation on the shores of the Baltic Sea.

From my eighth year onward annually I spent some weeks, later even months, by the seaside. The experience of the infinite bordering upon the finite, as one has it by the sea, responded to my tendency toward the border and supplied my imagination with a symbol from which feeling could win substance and thinking productivity.[3]

After his exile from Germany he found a retreat, again by the sea-shore, at the tip of Long Island. The sight of the great abyss refreshed his spirit and served as a recurrent sacrament of ultimate reality.

A particular place is naturally linked with a particular time. Dodd was, I think, specially conscious of critical turning-points in his own life of which his going to Oxford was perhaps the most significant. So he insisted that particularity within time is of perennial importance. Certain events within the history of Israel took place at divinely-ordained times (not fortuitously or as the result of human planning). The central event of all history came about in the fullness of time, at the time when the divine preparation of Israel and its neighbours had reached a proper stage, when the actualization of the divine purpose of redemption within human history became possible.

Over more than half a century Dodd clung to his conviction that the Son of God actually entered history in such a way that the ordinary flow of time was intersected by that which is in no way bound by time's regularities. He believed that the gospel records, though including much peripheral and extraneous material, contain a convincing testimony to events in the career of Jesus which actually happened in Palestine within a roughly datable time-span. It was essential, in his view, to affirm that the divine act of redemption could be located at a particular and critical point in the historical time-process: a general myth of redemption fails to convince the mind or engage the heart.

Thus the divine purpose for mankind came to decisive expression not exactly at a moment, though the moment of Jesus' death marks the turning point in a way which no other could do: that moment was central in a larger pattern of time-events – his birth, his initiation, his choice of disciples, his challenge to the authorities, his arrest, his crucifixion – a pattern which had been foreshadowed in the careers of Hebrew prophets but which had now come to final and decisive expression in the career of the Son of Man.

In a measure Muir and Eliot accept this view of time as containing within its steady flow intense moments of supreme significance. The moment when time 'stands still' is a moment to be celebrated above all others: history is a pattern of such 'timeless moments'. And the moment which is the still point of the whole universal drama is the moment of incarnation. Eliot summarized his own conviction when he wrote:

> Because I know that time is always time
> And place is always and only place
> And what is actual is actual only for one time
> And only for one place
> I rejoice that things are as they are.[4]

It is, however, in Tillich's philosophical system that the notion of the critical significance of a particular period of time becomes crucial. The 'period' may be a moment, a few minutes, a day, a year: its essential significance is that of a turning-point within whatever time-span is under consideration. Even before the First World War, largely as a result of his growing acquaintance with the writings of Schelling, Schopenhauer and Nietzsche he moved in theory towards a concentration upon existential moments in the history of mankind. But theory became a matter of personal experience on the Western Front and in his involvement in a shattered society after the war ended.

The personal *kairos* was for him a 'fulfilled moment, the moment of time approaching us as fate and decision'.[5] Even more dramatically, the turning-point in Germany's history at the end of the First World War he saw as a supreme *kairos* calling men to decision and action, to a 'daring interpretation of the present moment'.[6] It was crisis in human existence itself, an

> . . . experience lived through not only by Tillich himself, but by many of his generation in Germany at that time, all of them inspired and transported by the feeling that this was the crisis that could end only in new creation: Germany defeated, humiliated, punished for her saber-rattling overbearingness, shaken and purged and thereby enabled to bring to the world religious socialism, which the victorious nations, being all of them members of a disintegrating bourgeois world, needed no less than the defeated, but could not achieve precisely because of their victory.[7]

Such *kairoi* were indeed to be regarded as typical: there was however a unique *kairos* in the midst of time to which these lesser *kairoi* pointed and from which they derived their power. 'What happened in the unique *kairos*, the appearance of Jesus as the Christ, that is, as the center of history, may happen in derived form again and again, thus creating minor centers of importance.'[8] And although this doctrine raises many difficulties and needs to be viewed within Tillich's total interpretation of history, the main point that I am concerned to emphasize is that within his own experience and outlook the notion of critical turning-points in history became determinative, finding its unique and central expression in the Christ-event.

The sense of a particular time and place naturally leads to a concentration upon the nature of the event itself which happened in the particular space-time context. The simple title of one of Muir's poems is 'The Killing': this is the event of all human events which has startled and shocked the human imagination from the beginnings of recorded history. Even the killing of an animal can arouse grief and guilt and shame: the killing of a fellow human, especially if the relationship is intimate – a father, a wife, a son or daughter – stirs feelings of a far deeper intensity: the killing of the Son of God, if such can be conceived, is the most fearsome event of all. It is not surprising that those who have felt constrained to focus attention upon the particular have fastened upon the death of Jesus as constituting the central and most traumatic of all events which have happened in the world's history.

Dodd found it crucially significant in that it brought to climactic expression the visitations in judgment and mercy which had marked the recorded history of the Jewish people. Raven, vividly aware of the groaning and travailing which characterizes the whole process of evolution, saw in Jesus' heroic passive resistance of evil, even to death on the cross, the concrete particularity which illuminates and sanctifies the suffering of the total cosmos. For Muir, the killing was the breakthrough in what seemed otherwise to be an inexorable chain of retribution for evil deeds: nothing could have saved Bruce who killed Comyn except the death of One who reversed the entire order of retribution and raised a standard of hope even where law and death had reigned supreme. Place, time and action are held together in critical particularity in the lines:

> Did a God
> Indeed in dying cross my life that day?[9]

Eliot, in his most extended reference to the passion of Christ, chiefly emphasizes its perpetual operation throughout time. Nevertheless, he commits himself unequivocally to the faith that the healing energies of this continuing passion were transfused into the world's veins on a particular Friday through the sacrifice of a particular victim who was willing to give his flesh for our food, his blood for our drink and so to purify us from our infection, and restore us from our sickness.

> The dripping blood our only drink,
> The bloody flesh our only food:
> In spite of which we like to think
> That we are sound, substantial flesh and blood –
> Again, in spite of that, we call this Friday good.[10]

For Tillich, the cross stands as the central symbol not only of the New Testament but of his whole system. It is the symbol of the total self-sacrifice of finitude: it is the once-for-all negation of all finite ambitions and concerns. Yet he is careful not to isolate the cross completely within a kind of sacred vacuum. The symbol of the cross is given to men within the context of a story and that story gains meaning through other stories which both precede and follow the actual crucifixion of Jesus the Christ.

> The story of the Cross of Jesus as the Christ does not report an isolated event in his life but that event toward which the story of his life is directed and in which the others receive their meaning. Their meaning is that he who is the Christ subjects himself to the ultimate negativities of existence and that they are not able to separate him from his unity with God. Thus we find other symbols in the New Testament which point to and corroborate the more central symbol of the Cross of Jesus as the Christ.[11]

Having enumerated some of these preparatory and corroborative symbols Tillich concludes:

> All these . . . which could easily be multiplied and elaborated, are summed up in the symbol of the Cross. The Cross should not be separated from them, just as they should be interpreted in their totality as expressions of the subjection of him in whom the New Being is present to the conditions of existential estrangements. Whether these expressions are mythical, legendary, historical, or mixtures of all of them, they as well as the Cross, for which they are supporting symbols, are not important in themselves in the context of the biblical picture. They are important in their power to show the subjection of him who is the bearer of the New Being to the destructive structures of the old being.[12]

Thus a killing, which in its stark and callously inflicted form shocks us and shames us and shatters our complacency, becomes transfigured, when viewed as a willing submission to a law written into the very structure of the universe: the law that only through travail can new life come to birth, that only through self-renunciation can others receive grace, that only through the acceptance of an existing law's final sanction in death can the prospect of life under a new law become possible, that only through subjection to the destruction of the old being can the New Being be revealed. The key concept in all these metamorphoses is sacrifice. Sacrifice, in the sense of the willing surrender of a separate and secure existence to the possibilities of involvement in unknown perils, natural or social, has been widely acknowledged in human history as a pattern which is life-giving and life-enhancing. It is in addition the conviction of these five writers that this pattern has been supremely, definitively, decisively, particularly (no word is fully satisfactory if the act is unique) revealed in and through the death of Jesus the Christ. In him a killing has been translated into a supreme sacrifice. The killing has identifiable, historical features: sacrifice is the chief frame of interpretation which gives it eternal significance. Through the One the many find mercy and forgiveness: through the stripes of the One, the many are healed.

II

The interpretation which I have called centrifugal tries to penetrate beyond all phenomenal appearances in space and time to a reality which is transcendent and eternal. To be tied to any particular place was to Lawrence, for example, unthinkable. His evocations of the 'feel', the 'atmosphere', the 'spirit', of certain locations are magnificent but he was in fact always on the move, seeking the new place and the more satisfying environment. In the final section of his book on Lawrence, R. E. Pritchard shows, from direct quotations, how impossible Lawrence found it to stay for long in any one place. Germany, Italy, Ceylon, Australia, New Mexico – he tasted them all but found no abiding satisfaction in any one of them.

'This place no good'. This postscript to one of his last letters seems to epitomize the craving behind much of his career and writing. An exile since his early years, he sought always an impossible home: 'We travel, perhaps, with a secret and absurd hope of setting foot on the Hesperides, of running our boat up a little creek and landing it in the garden of Eden. This hope is always defeated. There is no Garden of Eden, and the Hesperides never were. Yet in our very search for them, we touch upon the coasts of illusion, and come into contact with other worlds.'[13]

Such an attitude is hardly surprising. He cherished the memory of the Nottinghamshire countryside, but had watched its slow erosion by the factory and the machine. He was devoted to England, but felt that its culture was dying as a result of the grievous wounds inflicted during the First World War. So he sought 'contact with other worlds' but found in them no place where he could for long feel at home. Wherever he went there were the same struggles between culture and anarchy, between the spirit and the flesh, between the civilized self and the savage beast. He imagined that he might find a place of reconciliation in America but the place was never found. He remained a displaced person to the end.

Similarly, though for different reasons, no place could hold more than a transitory significance for Stevens. His constant aim was to name the reality which he saw in the appearance: any physical structure and so any place could convey the real to the apprehending imagination. What was all-important was the interplay between the physical object exactly seen – the glistening steeple at Farmington, ordinary houses in New Haven, the shadow of Chocorua – and the imagination of the poet, an interplay which could issue in the naming process and the finished work of art. It is true that Stevens was pre-eminently the man of a particular place so far as his regular business life was concerned. A daily routine of body and mind tied him securely to his Hartford home and office, but this pattern had little relation, it seems, to the flight of his imagination. This, like a humming-bird, darted hither and thither, extracting treasures from every kind of physical object and transforming it into verbal patterns of dazzling beauty.

> We seek
> Nothing beyond reality, Within it,
>
> Everything, the spirit's alchemicana
> Included, the spirit that goes roundabout
> And through included, not merely the visible,
>
> The solid, but the movable, the moment,
> The coming on of feasts and the habits of saints,
> The patterns of the heavens and high, night air.[14]

Toynbee was deeply attached to a particular country from the very time when he first began to write. Greece became to him a second home, a land whose every feature he tried to explore and with whose total atmosphere he became increasingly familiar. But although there were innumerable sites and spots which had been hallowed by sacred traditions and legendary epiphanies, no one of these occupied for him any exclusive pre-eminence. The gods might appear here or there on earth: but their real dwelling-place was Olympus, the realm of light and spirit. Superb myths and dramas told of conjunctions in the commerce between heaven and earth, but there was no suggestion that any one of these was of critical significance. Toynbee shared the Greek feeling for the numinous and endeavoured to extend the limited Greek understanding of its manifestations. But this very projection on to a wider screen made it impossible for him to concentrate in any exclusive fashion upon a particular place or time in the realm of religious experience, even though, for example, he recorded an overpowering occasion in the chapel at Ampleforth. Spirit and matter were for him contrasting principles: they may interact but spirit cannot be confined within any material structure that can be identified within the process of human history.

And this seems to be true of Huxley who also imbibed from his earliest years the spirit of classical Greece. His special interests turned eventually to the world of living creatures and to the evidences which the natural order provides of an evolutionary pattern governing the onward movement of the universal life-process. He wrote movingly of experiences which he enjoyed, experiences which exalted him to a sense of identity with the total cosmos, moments when he felt mystically united with nature in all its wonder and beauty. But such experiences could in no way be confined to particular places and times. He could vividly remember when and where they occurred: in a place maybe where colour and fragrance and light assailed the senses with unusually persuasive power or at a time when harmony of sound made a peculiar impact upon his musical awareness. Yet the place and the time were in a sense fortuitous. The uplifting sense of transcendence came not through relationship to the divine embodied within space-time phenomena but through a sudden conjunction of opposites – the spirit of man and the world of nature united within a momentary flash of recognition which produced in the human psyche a mixture of feelings – fear, wonder, admiration – which together erupt into the experience of religious awe.

In a fine expression of his essentially centrifugal outlook Huxley once wrote:

> I believe that the great sacrifice needed for religion (i.e. traditional religion) is that of her old certitude, to be offered up on the altar of humility. And that demanded by organized science is that of all narrowness and aggressiveness to be offered on the altar of reverence and imaginative love.[15]

Humility and openness in face of the immensities and the profundities of the universe and of the works of man's creation – this, in Huxley's view, is a true religious humanism, the only acceptable religion for humanity today.

Perhaps of the five centrifugal attitudes which I have noted that of Jaspers is the most explicitly opposed to any concentration upon a particular revelation of the transcendent in space and time. This opposition assumed dramatic personal expression in his encounters with Rudolf Bultmann. These two, who became giants in German academic circles from 1920 onwards, had been boys together in school, Jaspers being roughly one year senior in age. In contrast to Jaspers' home circle which was inspired by a liberal and rational humanism, Bultmann's background was that of Lutheran piety and evangelistic zeal. The older boy claimed later to have seen already in the playground of the Gymnasium a certain gleam in the young Bultmann's eye which half attracted him yet kept him at a distance. And when in 1920 Bultmann came to lecture at Heidelberg, where Jaspers had been installed as Professor, the distance became far more pronounced. Jaspers likened Bultmann to 'an immovable block of granite'. He felt that real contact had become impossible. Though the two men entered into a friendly dialogue concerning Bultmann's policy of demythologizing the Christian tradition, there proved to be no real point of meeting. That God could localize himself in a unique way and that this localization could be expressed through space-time categories was for Jaspers an utterly unacceptable notion.

In point of fact, Bultmann himself was little concerned about space categories; but that a saving event had actually happened within the time-series was an indispensable part of his message. This did not imply, he urged, any fixing of God as an object but it did imply that it was now possible for man to be related to God by a faith-act connected with the one saving event. This faith-act needed constantly to be renewed *in actu* and *pro me*. Such acts of faith, wherever made, had only become a possibility because of the divine initiative in the saving event of the cross.

Such a doctrine of particularity was entirely foreign to Jaspers' own experience and philosophical outlook. In his own experience there was no strong sense of guilt or estrangement needing to be removed: life for him had been a process of growth and expansion. There had indeed been tensions through self-consciousness and difficulties in self-communication, problems which could be paralleled on the wider stage of human history by what he came to call axial or pivotal developments – the kind of change which he associated specially with the era around the middle of the last millennium BC when in China, India, Persia, Israel and Greece religious and philosophical works were composed which have ever since continued to influence mankind. 'Incarnations of the ideal', 'ciphers' of ultimate reality in space-time formulations, Jaspers could allow. But any thought of a single, determinative, condensed revelation was contrary to his whole philosophical outlook.

A favourite metaphor of Jaspers is that drawn from the process of breaking through an encompassing shell into a world of richer reality. It is a centrifugal image. Life is expansiveness, not necessarily steady and continuous, but constantly related to the breaking through of existential constrictions into realms of ever-widening experience. There must, it is true, be specializations but never as ends in themselves. The horizon, and new distances, ever beckoned him on. 'The uncharted and inexhaustible Encompassing surrounds all our horizons and can be thought of as the background of all backgrounds.'[16] His response was a faith which he called philosophical but which from many points of view could surely have been called religious.

III

Any attempt to identify a turning-point in human history is a precarious enterprise. But more than half a century has passed since the decade 1910–20 and there are many reasons to suggest that within that decade, at least as far as the Western world is concerned, a change of almost unparalleled significance took place. There was change in the external structures of society brought about by the 1914–18 War and by the Communist Revolution. There was the change in the inner-consciousness of man brought about by the impact of Freudian psychology, of relativity-theory, of rapid technological advance. And it was during this decade that all the writers whose works I have considered reached the age when a man normally regards his years of preparation as ended and gains confidence to express his own point of view.

All had been deeply influenced by the general climate of thought and by the accepted social conventions in which they had been reared. In broad terms the nineteenth century had been the heyday of idealism, romanticism, liberalism, moralism: the twentieth century was destined to move steadily towards realism, materialism, determinism, positivism. Somehow the 'religious' man had to find a place in between. At first sight the nineteenth-century atmosphere might have seemed the more congenial to the life of religion but could its division between spirit and matter be sustained? Could a 'religion' dominantly concerned with ideals and moral absolutes have any bearing upon the crises and problems which were affecting the life of twentieth-century man? On the other hand, the acceptance of an unqualified materialism or determinism would appear to render the very notion of 'religion' obsolete.

It is possible, I think, to see our first group of writers as men reacting from any purely idealist conception of religion, and of Christianity in particular. Raven, for example, made a close study of the Platonic framework which governed the formulation of early Alexandrian theology but rejected its abstractions in favour of the more down-to-earth approach of the school of Antioch. Yet he was not content simply to sift historical evidence and regard the residue as a deposit of general religious experience. Through careful examinations of personal testimonies, enshrined in the available texts, he came to discern ever more clearly the portrait of an historical figure going about Galilee and going good, coming ultimately to Jerusalem to suffer and to die. Moreover, through observing the lives of those engaged in works of social compassion, he came also to recognize that same presence in his own contemporary world. So to him the Christ became neither a purely ideal conception nor just an eminent figure in history but rather a personal presence, revealed both through historical incarnation and through present living relationships. The larger emphasis doubtless was upon the massive witness of the New Testament, particularly that of St Paul, but Raven's was never a bare factual historicism. Past and present were held together in what seemed to him an integrating balance. Each served to make more vivid the constraining presence of the One who called and still calls, who brought and still brings saving grace to mankind.

Dodd devoted himself more fully than any of the other authors I have named to disciplined and detailed examination of ancient texts.

At times it may seem that the result of his labours was the identification of a message rather than the delineation of a man. Yet he never wavered in his conviction that the existence of the message is inconceivable apart from the man. And that the man, conversely, is known not simply as an isolated figure, some of whose words and deeds have been preserved, but as a personal presence who continues to reveal himself to successive generations through the constant re-enactment in word and deed of his saving message.

> What emerges (i.e. from the documents) is a lively picture of the *kind* of thing that Jesus did, the *kind* of attitude which his actions revealed, the *kind* of relations in which he stood with various types of people he encountered, and the causes of friction between him and the religious leaders. The question, how far this or that story may be taken as an accurate account of what happened on this or that occasion is one upon which judgments will vary. Some, as they stand, may be found more credible than others. One or the other may be felt not to be in character. But taken together, these stories, told from many different points of view, converge to give a distinct impression of a real person in action upon a recognizable scene.[17]

God's purpose to redeem mankind was, I think, Dodd's guiding star throughout his intellectual pilgrimage. But it was never enough for him to pursue it as a remote transcendent ideal. He believed that the purpose had become part of the very stuff of human history in and through the saving mission of Jesus of Nazareth. In him the final goal had come to real though incomplete manifestation. Thereafter the purpose continued to be worked out as the Spirit interpreted and re-enacted that which had taken place at the centre of the time-process.

It might be argued that Dodd relied too heavily upon what can be deduced from the records of ancient history: in the dialectic between past and present, the past for him undoubtedly played the dominant role. In the cases of Eliot and Muir the bias is in the other direction. Eliot grew up in the atmosphere of New England transcendentalism and idealism but this at length proved to be too rare and refined for his soul's health. He needed relationships with the real world, with a longer historical tradition, with a broader range of social experience. Yet the city of London and primitive mythology and Sweeney could not by themselves mediate the ultimate reality which he was ever seeking. Mere curiosity, searching past and future, was an escape from reality. The saints, as he now realized, had devoted themselves through

> a lifetime's death in love,
> Ardour and selflessness and self-surrender

to the apprehension of

> The point of intersection of the timeless
> With time.

To most of us indeed there come only 'hints and guesses' of this critical moment. But in fact

> The hint half guessed, the gift half understood, is
>   Incarnation.
> Here the impossible union
> Of spheres of existence is actual,
> Here the past and future
> Are conquered, and reconciled.[18]

Only through a real meeting, at a particular place and time, could the clashes and contraries of ordinary human experience be sacramentally resolved.

Idealism and legalism easily go hand in hand. It was the rigid logic and predestinarianism of his Calvinist upbringing that Edwin Muir rejected and for a long time this left him exposed to the varied seductions of utopian, nihilist, socialist and marxist theories. But at length he discovered a source of integration and healing in a form of Christianity which had been purged of its hard moralistic injunctions. He returned to the Christ of the New Testament and found in the old familiar stories the inspiration for some of his finest poems. The transfiguration of the Christ was a parable of that which could happen to any man at any time. That Christ had actually walked this earth he came firmly to believe but he was never content to hold this truth in isolation: even more important was the truth that his living presence continued to be manifested through word and image and dramatic action, transfiguring the common life of men and restoring to them the paradise to which otherwise there could have been no return.

The rejection of idealism is dramatically illustrated in Tillich's philosophical career. His early training had been in the classical German tradition of Kant, Hegel and Schelling. The last-named attracted him most of all but already in his writings he found suggestions of those contradictions which were incompatible with a pure idealism. Then, however, the war and the events following the war in central Europe made it impossible for him to retain any kind of romantic, idealistic philosophy. 'War and revolution have revealed depths of reality which idealism cannot master.' 'It does not see the abyss which opens before every time and every present.'[19]

No system could satisfy him which did not offer some way of resolving the cleavage between essence and existence, the estrangement between the unconditioned and alienated mankind. This resolution he found not primarily in a bare event or even in a well-defined career but rather through a picture – the picture of the New Being in Jesus the Christ. The picture was derived from the gospel portraits but it could not be reproduced in detail with scientific exactitude. Man could stand before the picture and be grasped by it and in the process overcome his estrangement and participate in the New Being. Tillich never ceased to magnify the place of reason, the logos, in human life but knew that there were times when no appeal to reason could suffice. In the depths only faith, the courage to be, the acceptance of grace, could constitute the way of salvation. And this 'faith' was to be regarded not simply as a leap into a void: it gained both direction and dynamic by its relation to the picture or image which had become a part of human history through the career of Jesus of Nazareth.

Turning to the group of what I have called centrifugal writers, it is possible to regard each as recoiling from the positivistic tendencies of his time, whether in the realm of history or science or the arts. Toynbee refused to accept as a valid description of the historian's task the mere assembling and organizing of 'the facts' (analogous to that of an industrialist with his 'raw materials'). Facts are not like boulders strewn along the historian's way.

They are like flaked and chopped flints, hewn stones or bricks. Human action has had a hand in making them what they are . . . Facts are, in truth, exactly what is meant by the Latin word *facta* from which the English word is derived. They are 'things that have been made' – that is to say 'fictitious' things rather than 'factual' things . . . For this reason it is quite inappropriate to regard history as being a sequence of facts, and the historian's job as being merely to accumulate as great a number of facts as he can muster . . . History is the framing of questions by a particular human being in a particular space-time context; he asks questions, and he adduces evidence to support his answers, and in both these cases he makes use of hypothesis before ever he 'finds' a fact.[20]

But, allowing for 'fictions' and 'hypotheses', does it then follow that 'your guess is as good as mine' and that an accumulation of objective facts is to be replaced simply by a collection of subjective hypotheses? This alternative Toynbee refused to accept. He clung to the conviction that there are clear evidences of patterns in universal history, particularly in relation to the phenomenon of death to which individuals and (in a less obvious sense) societies are alike subject. Is death the end of all things? It may be. But for himself Toynbee found sufficient support in his study of history for the hypotheses of restoration and reintegration and rebirth and reunion to justify him in the faith that beyond all this-worldly phenomena there exists a spiritual and eternal reality with which man himself can be united in freedom and trust. The great religions, he affirmed, all testify 'that the cause of sin and suffering and sorrow is the separation of sentient beings, in their brief passage through the phenomenal world, from the timeless reality behind the phenomena, and that a reunion with this reality is the sole but sovereign cure for our ailing world's ills.'[21] He could not accept the 'exclusive' claims of Christian orthodoxy but regarded certain Christian visions of ultimate spiritual reality as sublime expressions of what that reality actually is.

Lawrence, though he rebelled against the kind of hard mechanical rationalism associated with modern industry, and the deterministic systems associated with some forms of modern science, regarded the Christianity he had known as too anaemic, too intellectualized, too muted, to serve as an alternative. He wanted a religion but it must include the 'shaggy', the 'horrible', the 'awful', the 'splendid', above all the power-full. 'We're sick of being soft and amiable and harmless.'[22] He saw another side of Christianity in the Apocalypse and dreamed that a new religion might yet be born out of the union of love and power, the feminine and the masculine, in some hoped-for future age. But the unceasing conflict of opposites within the ongoing surge of life captivated his imagination and made any thought of resolution within a historic Christ-figure impossible. Reacting violently against all closed systems, he sought a religion which would give free expression to passion, the blood, the fire. He did not despise or dismiss the Christ of his early chapel-going experiences. But in *The Man Who Died* he gave a complete transmutation, even parody, of the man who lived in Nazareth and died upon a cross.

Not ideas, not theories, not even facts: Lawrence's passionate concern was for life and a religion of life. However romanticized his picture

of the Etruscans and their religion may have been, it clearly expressed
that for which he yearned and hoped.

> To the Etruscans all was alive; the whole universe lived; and the
> business of man was himself to live amid it all. He had to draw life
> into himself, out of the wandering huge vitalities of the world. The
> cosmos was alive, like a vast creature . . . The whole thing was alive,
> and had a great soul . . . and in spite of one great soul, there were
> myriad roving, lesser souls; every man, every creature and tree and
> lake and mountain and stream, was animate, and had its own peculiar
> consciousness.[23]

With such a vision of life, a concentration like Eliot's upon a unique
incarnation at a particular moment in time was for him unthinkable.
'God is the great urge that has not yet found a body but urges towards
incarnation with the great creative urge. And becomes at last a clove
carnation: lo! that is god!'

No one, surely, in the twentieth century has celebrated the wonder of
life with such enthusiasm and such abandon. He could not abide the
attempts to enclose life within the neat package of evolutionary theory.
Life was for ever changing. Nothing was ever finished. The language
by which he describes the poetry which extols life in the immediate
present is dazzling. 'The seething poetry of the incarnate Now', 'its
quivering momentaneity', 'swifter than iridescence, haste, not rest,
come-and-go, not fixity, inconclusiveness, immediacy, the quality of
life itself without *dénouement*, without close'. And the quality of life is
that of 'running flame', 'the very white quick of nascent creation'; 'A
water-lily heaves herself from the flood, looks round, gleams and is
gone. We have seen the incarnation, the quick of the ever-swirling
flood.'[24] Religion is in fact the celebration of life: nothing more, nothing less. And life has no bounds, no crystallizations To give vocal
expression to what he could 'feel in my running blood' was the sum and
substance of Lawrence's religion.

Of Stevens and his philosophy of life it is not easy to write with confidence. Whereas Lawrence the man is vividly present in all his writing,
Stevens remains a mysterious figure in the background – the poetry,
the sheer beauty of the words is everything. The Real exists: like the
sun it draws every energy of the human imagination towards itself: at
the same time the imagination retreats baffled, possessing no adequate
language to express what it has seen. So Stevens employs phrase after
phrase from his amazingly varied verbal store. He tries mode after

mode; he rings the changes on grammar and syntax: nothing is solid or
fixed. There are affirmations and counter-affirmations; hypotheses and
refutations: theories and contradictions. At one moment reality is
named – and immediately it is gone. Only the poem remains. The
quintessential poem, the all-embracing poem, can never be written by
any man. But as we yield ourselves to the illumination and the reson-
ance of any single poem we gain a momentary awareness of ultimate
reality.

'Notes Toward a Supreme Fiction' is Stevens' most ambitious poem,
though the very title expresses the poet's recognition of his own
limitations. It would be possible to make an interesting comparison between this title and that of T. S. Eliot's book *Notes Towards the Definition
of Culture*, which appeared at roughly the same time. The comparison
aptly illustrates the distinction that I am making between the centripetal
and the centrifugal, for whereas Eliot's title suggests a concentration
within certain limits, Stevens' title invites the imagination to expand
towards the Unlimited. For him the ultimate is 'a reality that forces
itself upon our consciousness and refuses to be managed and mastered',
'something "wholly other" by which the inexpressible loneliness of
thinking is broken and enriched'.[25] This reality is revealed by the poet
in so far as he gains insight into reality and expresses it through a
'fiction'.

This fiction, however, always falls short of the 'supreme fiction'
which would be the perfect union of imagination and reality. So man
is condemned to the 'incessant conjunctionings' of imagination and
reality, though in another sense this dialectic constitutes the very excite-
ment and satisfaction of his life. Stevens spent his working days in the
context of legal abstractions and mathematical calculations and he never
ceased to value the formal structures which made an orderly human
existence possible. But these were not the media through which reality
could be approached. Whatever information experimental science or
abstract reason could provide they could not cover particularity here
and now.

Poetry has to do with reality in that concrete and individual aspect of
it which the mind can never tackle altogether on its own terms, with
matter that is foreign and alien in a way in which abstract systems,
ideas in which we detect an inherent pattern, a structure that belongs
to the ideas themselves, can never be . . . its function, the need which
it meets and which has to be met in some way in every age that is not

to become decadent or barbarous is precisely this contact with reality as it impinges on us from the outside, the sense that we can touch and feel a solid reality which does not wholly dissolve itself into the conceptions of our own minds. It is the individual and particular that does this.[26]

To know facts as facts, to discover rational connections – these disciplines have their place. But the wonder and mystery of art is to discover by imagination the unity rooted in the individuality of objects, to become aware of 'the irrevocability by which a thing is what it is'.

It is the calling and high dignity of the poet, then, to be the one who through imagination, can reach out most authentically towards that Reality which could only be fully expressed by the Supreme Fiction. He does not seek for an incarnation in history or in nature but rather uses any individual object in the ever-changing world as the springboard by which his imagination can leap into the unknown and create a fiction which is a partial revelation of the Real.

It is here that the affinity of art and religion is most evident to-day. Both have to mediate for us a reality not ourselves. This is what the poet does. The supreme virtue here is humility, for the humble are they that move about the world with the love of the real in their hearts.[27]

Jaspers' dissatisfaction with a purely rational and scientific approach to reality arose in a different way. No one could have accused him of denigrating reason and scientific discipline. His earliest years were spent in a context in which there was a constant appeal to reason: his long course in the study of medicine involved him daily in the scientific investigation of phenomena. He wanted to know actuality and this seemed the altogether promising way.

But in all this, he once wrote, 'the basic question viz. how one ought to live, remained unsolved'. Could reason deal with the ultimate situations in which every man sooner or later finds himself engulfed? Could science and scientific theories ever encompass the whole man? 'The totality of man lies way beyond any conceivable objectifiability. He is incompletable both as a being-for-himself and as an object of cognition. He remains, so to speak, "open". Man is always more than what he knows, or can know, about himself.' In spite of all attempts by scientists to provide rational explanations, the origin of life, the appearance of man, the emergence of self-consciousness, the freedom of the individual, remained unsolved mysteries.

Yet Jaspers never rejected the way of science. 'Scientific knowledge', he affirmed, 'is an indispensable factor in all philosophizing. Without science no veracity is possible to-day . . . Science, on the other hand, cannot understand why it itself exists. It does not reveal the meaning of life . . . It has limits of which it is itself aware insofar as it is clearly conscious of its methods.' Hence there had to be a second type of thinking to which he devoted himself with equal seriousness. It was the type which 'confronts me with myself', which focusses attention upon 'the philosophizing person, his basic experiences, his actions, his world, his everyday conduct, the forces which speak through him', and perhaps most of all upon his ways of communicating with "the other". 'Interlinkage of self-existent persons (supremely realized for Jaspers in his relations with his wife) constitutes the invisible reality of the essential.'[28] In this second type of thinking one problem became of paramount importance – the problem of freedom.

> The basic problem of our time is whether an independent human being in his self-comprehended destiny is still possible. Indeed, it has become a general problem whether man can be free – and this is a problem which, as clearly formulated and understood, tends to annul itself: for only he who is capable of being free can sincerely and comprehendingly moot the problem of freedom.[29]

Jaspers clung to the conviction that man could be free and the obverse of this conviction was that man is encompassed by transcendent forces which draw him out from the enclosedness of his world and of himself. Transcendence can never be objectified and reflected in a human body of knowledge but in his existential experiences man constantly responds to that which is from beyond and in that response tastes freedom. 'God exists for me in the degree to which I in freedom authentically become myself. He does not exist as a scientific content but only as an openness to *Existenz*.'[30]

Jaspers could never accept the particularity of the Christian tradition. But he became an eager student of the Bible and found in the witness of the Hebrew prophets to transcendence the essence of his own philosophical faith. The prohibition of any kind of image of deity he extended to include all attempts to systematize knowledge of the transcendent. God is known only in and through the power by which he enables man to leap out into freedom, to soar towards the all-encompassing. During the dark and threatening days of the Nazi regime Jaspers and his wife continually found comfort and courage through reading the stories of the prophets. Again and again he returned to the words spoken by Jeremiah to Baruch at a time of desolation, finding there a supreme illustration of the fact that when a man is confident in God he does not despair even in what seems to be final desolation. His comment on this passage: 'That God is, is enough. When all things fade away, God is – that is the only fixed point' is surely the comment of a deeply religious man. His studies in the realms of natural science, of history, of psychology, of art, he regarded as necessary for the understanding of his world but none could give him either the sense of reality as a whole or the power to 'soar' towards that reality. Through 'faith' he responded to the transcendent wonder of the all-encompassing: by means of constantly renewed decisions he sought to overcome the threat of what he called the 'ultimate situations' – guilt and suffering and nothingness and death.

IV

What conclusions can we finally draw from this brief survey of the lives and writings of these outstanding men who, each in his own way, left a mark upon the first half of the twentieth century? All shared the conviction that the universe of their experience cannot be explained or interpreted as a closed system in which living creatures and lifeless objects merely rattle around, acting and reacting upon one another in fortuitous and meaningless ways: all agreed that however adept man may become at controlling and organizing his immediate environment, natural and social, he still needs to come to terms with what is referred to sometimes as mystery, sometimes as spiritual presence, sometimes as reality, sometimes as creator spirit, sometimes as the numinous, sometimes as the transcendent, sometimes as God. There may be less assurance about how far every man possesses what may be called a religious sense or a sixth sense or a concern for the ultimate, but so far as their own individual experiences were concerned its existence seemed indubitable.

If there was so much agreement, wherein did the main difference of opinion or conviction finally lie? Not in any contrast between their varying life-interests and professional occupations: I have chosen pairs united in their devotion to historical studies, to the life-sciences, to poetry and drama, to philosophy. Not altogether in the circumstances of their social and religious upbringing, though these in each case exercised a profound influence upon the mature man: their backgrounds include upper-class, middle-class, lower-class: the law, teaching, farming, mining, social service all are represented. Perhaps the most obvious difference is that in the home and family situations of what I have called the centripetal group there was a far greater emphasis than in the centrifugal group upon regular Bible reading and upon Sunday worship. In the one group a sustained effort was made to initiate children into the Christian tradition whereas, in the other, formal expressions of religion existed within a dominantly humanistic system of values. It is true that in Raven's case the pattern of family life was mainly geared to the inculcation of Christian values and that in the case of Lawrence there was in his earliest years a good deal of chapel-going and thereby the boy became familiar with certain parts of the Bible and with gospel hymns. Yet, in general, on the one side of the comparison Christian faith and practice was the norm of community life, on the other side religion was valued as the support of morals and the ally of aesthetic sensitivities.

At a later stage, the members of the first group reveal themselves as the more acutely aware of radical evil in the world. Raven and Tillich were both deeply scarred by their experiences in the trenches during the First World War on opposite sides of the firing line. Eliot faced in imagination the horrors of the Wasteland, depression and war, and tried to identify the contradictions of human experience. Muir endured a purgatorial trial through his exposure to the social dereliction of sections of Glasgow. Later, too, he went through the agony of seeing the Czechoslovakia, which he had come to love, being dismembered before his very eyes. Dodd's life seems to have been more protected from the social evils of his own time but he was well enough aware of the history of human conflicts and alienations, particularly as they figure in the stories of the Old Testament. His intimate acquaintance with the scriptures left him in no doubt that divine judgment was a grim reality, the inevitable reaction of goodness to man's perennial grasping for prestige and possessions and power.

In the writings of the second group I find less emphasis on this kind of radical evil or on human antagonisms. Huxley was aware of the stultifying effects of human pride and ignorance, Toynbee of man's weakness and vacillations in face of the challenges which cannot be avoided in this world. Stevens and Lawrence, too, while recognizing the imperfections of human responses to the grandeur and dynamism inherent in every manifestation of life, saw this characteristic of humanity more as defect than as defiance, more as a limitation to be overcome than as a refusal to be reversed. Jaspers, though he and his wife experienced dark and threatening circumstances, continued to believe that temporary dislocations and aberrations would be transcended and that humanity could continue to move towards its true destiny.

This difference of attitude in estimating the nature of man and of his involvement in suffering and evil was reflected in a comparable difference of outlook concerning the nature of the divine and of its relation both to the world and to human affairs. On the one side were those who, while gladly recognizing that divine reality was mediated to the human consciousness in richly variegated ways, were convinced that these manifestations indicate personal activity and that through the agency of a particular personal presence, acting in space and time, this mediation had gained unique expression and effectiveness. It did not follow that any single testimony to this central revelation could be definitive or final: the multiple insights and images of scientist, poet and historian all have a part to play. But the notable fact remains that in and through them all there is a convergence of vision and testimony towards a personal Christ-figure who is identifiable with the Christ of the New Testament, the Christ involved in suffering and the victim of evil, the Christ of past and present reconciling activity. He is, they believed, the One through whom the eternal and ultimately mysterious God has visited and redeemed a people whose destiny it now becomes to share his image and to continue his mission.

On the other side were those who recognized and celebrated transcendent mystery or spiritual reality, manifested in and through the myriad movements and transmutations and inter-relations of terrestrial phenomena: appearing here, appearing there: by one observed in this way, by another in that way: expressible to a degree through human symbolic forms, but never in ways suggesting the particularity and singularity and distinctiveness of personal decisive action, yet always inviting the earth-bound to pierce beyond phenomenal appearances to ultimate ineffable reality.

These two interpretations of man's relation to transcendence can perhaps be summarized in two words: *reconciliation* (central e.g. in the system of Paul Tillich) and *fulfilment* (a favourite e.g. in the memories of Julian Huxley). Man, when conscious of his estrangement, alienation, guilt, responds to the message of reconciliation: when conscious of his limitations, frustrations, unrealized ambitions, stretches out towards fulfilment. To illustrate the first I choose part of Edwin Muir's poem, 'The Church' in which he uses the central Christian symbol, the cross, to express his faith in the possibility of a universal reconciliation through the revelation of the One whom he called the 'turning-point of time and the meaning of life'. To illustrate the second I shall quote a beautiful passage from *The Rainbow* in which one of D. H. Lawrence's favourite symbols, the arch, is used to direct the imagination upwards towards a satisfying fulfilment.

In the poem 'The Church' Muir recalls an event which he had witnessed, probably in New England, on one of his American visits. About the church as a great institution in history, its wealth and its dogmatism, he raises serious questions and doubts in the second half of the poem; but in the first part his gaze is directed towards the symbol, the new cross crowning the still unfinished church.

> Someone inside me sketches a cross – askew,
> A child's – on seeing that stick crossed with a stick,
> Some simple ancestor, perhaps, that knew,
> Centuries ago when all were Catholic,
> That this archaic trick
> Brings to the heart and the fingers what was done
> One spring day in Judaea to Three in One;
>
> When God and Man in more than love's embrace,
> Far from their heaven and tumult died,
> And the holy Dove fluttered above that place
> Seeking its desolate nest in the broken side,
> And Nature cried
> To see Heaven doff its glory to atone
> For man, lest he should die in time, alone.[31]

In *The Rainbow* Tom Brangwen falls in love with and marries Lydia, the widow of Paul Lensky who had been killed in the war, and the mother already of one child, Anna. Did this mean divided loyalties? The narrative reads:

> What was Paul Lensky to her, but an unfilled possibility to which he, Brangwen, was the reality and the fulfilment? What did it matter, that Anna Lensky was born of Lydia and Paul? God was her father and her mother. He had passed through the married pair without fully making Himself known to them. Now He was declared to Brangwen and to Lydia Brangwen, as they stood together. When at

last they had joined hands, the house was finished, and the Lord took up His abode. And they were glad . . .

Anna's soul was put at peace between them. She looked from one to the other, and she saw them established to her safety, and she was free. She played between the pillar of fire and the pillar of cloud in confidence, having the assurance on her right hand and the assurance on her left. She was no longer called upon to uphold with her childish might the broken end of the arch. Her father and her mother now met to the span of the heavens, and she; the child, was free to play in the space beneath, between.[32]

The centripetal, concentrated revelation through the *Word*: the Word spoken through men and supremely through the Man: the centrifugal, expansive life of the *Spirit*, the Spirit animating the life of the whole universe and above all inspiring the upsoaring aspirations of mankind. Must we settle for one *or* the other? Yes, if the interpreters of reconciliation refuse to allow for even the possibility of experiences of at-one-ment in man's life in the natural order and in his social relationships. Yes, if the interpreters of fulfilment refuse to allow for even the possibility of a supreme concentration of spiritual energy in and through a central personal career in space and time. But must such exclusivist claims be made? Is truth to be found in monologue, in uniformity, in the single vision, through the one-track mind? Or is it to be found through dialogue, through dialectic, through mutual interchange, even through the juxtaposition of contraries?

All life, so far as we know, can be represented only in terms of structure *and* energy. All communication, so far as we know, can be represented only in terms of form *and* meaning. The life of the Godhead, according to the long-established trinitarian confession, includes both the form of Sonship *and* the energy of the Spirit. Is it then surprising that no exclusive pattern of human testimony can ever fully encompass the mystery of that ultimate Reality whose incarnate form is that of personal reconciling activity and whose creative energy directs the whole universe on towards its true fulfilment?

NOTES

Chapter 2 C. H. Dodd and Arnold Toynbee

1. C. H. Dodd, *History and the Gospel*, James Nisbet 1938, pp. 27ff.
2. Ibid., p. 37.
3. Ibid., p. 36.
4. Arnold Toynbee, *Experiences*, OUP 1969, p. 90.
5. Ibid., p. 108.
6. Ibid., p. 132.
7. Ibid., p. 135.
8. Arnold Toynbee, *A Study of History*, 12 vols, OUP 1935–61.
9. Arnold Toynbee in *The Listener*, 2 April 1970, p. 439.
10. C. H. Dodd, *The Bible Today*, CUP 1946.
11. C. H. Dodd, *The Founder of Christianity*, Collins 1971, pp. 170f.
12. Toynbee, *A Study of History*, Vol 9, OUP 1954, pp. 634–7.

Chapter 3 C. E. Raven and Julian Huxley

1. Julian Huxley, *Memories*, Allen & Unwin 1970, p. 20.
2. Ibid., p. 73.
3. C. E. Raven, *Science, Religion and the Future*, CUP 1943, p. 111.
4. Julian Huxley, *Religion without Revelation*, James Watts & Co. 1941, p. 7.
5. Ibid., p. 46.
6. Ibid., p. 83.
7. In the Preface to *Religion without Revelation*.
8. Huxley, *Memories*, pp. 153f.
9. C. E. Raven, *Evolution and the Christian Concept of God*, OUP 1936, p. 21.
10. Ibid., pp. 30f.
11. C. E. Raven, *Creator Spirit*, Martin Hopkinson & Co. 1927, p. 236.
12. C. E. Raven, *A Wanderer's Way*, Martin Hopkinson & Co. 1928, p. 78.
13. C. E. Raven, *Good News of God*, Hodder 1945, pp. 48f.
14. I discovered this letter amongst Charles Raven's papers. when working on his biography.
15. Reprinted in *Contemporary Religious Issues* ed. D. E Hartsock, Wadsworth Publishing Co., California 1968, pp. 182ff.
16. Julian Huxley, *Memories 2*, Allen & Unwin 1973.
17. C. E. Raven, *The Quest of Religion*, SCM Press 1928, pp. 55f.

Chapter 4 Edwin Muir and Wallace Stevens

1. Stevens died in August 1955.

2. *Letters of Wallace Stevens* ed. Holly Stevens, Faber 1967, p. 14.

3. Ibid., p. 29.

4. Ibid., pp. 58f.

5. Ibid., pp. 139f.

6. Roy Fuller, *Owls and Artificers: Oxford Lectures on Poetry*, André Deutsch 1971, p. 72.

7. Edwin Muir, *An Autobiography*, Hogarth Press 1954, p. 246.

8. Edwin Muir, 'The Transfiguration', *Collected Poems*, Faber 1964, pp. 198f.

9. Edwin Muir, 'Robert the Bruce: To Douglas in Dying', *Collected Poems*, pp. 115f.

10. From the central section of 'Notes toward a Supreme Fiction', *The Collected Poems of Wallace Stevens*, Faber 1955, p. 392.

11. In *Yale Review*, Vol LIX, 1968, p. 288.

12. *The Collected Poems of Wallace Stevens*, p. 529.

13. Muir, *An Autobiography*, p. 281.

14. Muir, *Collected Poems*, p. 227.

Chapter 5   *T. S. Eliot and D. H. Lawrence*

1. T. S. Eliot, *The Idea of a Christian Society*, Faber 1939, p. 62.

2. Martin Jarrett-Kerr, *D. H. Lawrence and Human Existence*, SCM Press 1961, with a Foreword by T. S. Eliot; first issued 1951 by Rockliffe Publishing Corporation under the author's pen name, William Tiverton. In the appendix to his book *D. H. Lawrence: Novelist* (Chatto 1955, Penguin 1970), F. R. Leavis makes a spirited defence of Lawrence against Eliot's insinuations.

3. *The Letters of D. H. Lawrence* ed. Aldous Huxley, Heinemann 1932, p. 190.

4. Djuna Barnes, *Nightwood*, Faber 1936, has a Preface by T. S. Eliot.

5. F. R. Leavis (with Q. D. Leavis), *Lectures in America*, Chatto 1969, p. 45.

6. Autobiographical Sketch in *Phoenix II: Uncollected, Unpublished and Other Prose Works by D. H. Lawrence* ed. Warren Roberts and Harry T. Moore, Heinemann 1968, p. 592.

7. Article in *Phoenix II*, p. 600.

8. D. H. Lawrence, *Sons and Lovers*, Heinemann 1913: Phoenix edn 1956, p. 256.

9. Reprinted in D. H. Lawrence, *Selected Literary Criticism* ed. Anthony Beale, Heinemann 1955, p. 167.

10. *The Collected Letters of D. H. Lawrence* ed. Harry T. Moore, Heinemann 1962, Vol I, p. 280.

11. D. H. Lawrence, *The Rainbow*, Heinemann 1915; Phoenix edn 1971, p. 496.

12. *Phoenix II*, pp. 598f.

13. *Collected Letters*, Vol I, p. 40.

14. *Phoenix: The Posthumous Papers of D. H. Lawrence* ed. Edward D. MacDonald, Heinemann 1961, p. 528. By 'religion', Lawrence probably means theology.

15. 'Burnt Norton' II, *Four Quartets*, in *Collected Poems 1909–1962*, Faber 1963, p. 191.

16. In *Selected Prose*, Penguin 1953, pp. 85f.
17. In his Introduction to *The Letters of D. H. Lawrence*.

Chapter 6 Paul Tillich and Karl Jaspers

1. Karl Jaspers, 'Philosophical Autobiography'; written for the volume *The Philosophy of Karl Jaspers* ed. P. A. Schilpp and translated by the editor, The Library of Living Philosophy, Tudor Publishing Co., NY 1957, p. 8.
2. Ibid., p. 12.
3. Ibid., p. 19.
4. Paul Tillich, *The Interpretation of History*, Scribners, NY 1936, p. 3.
5. He was born in a village about seventy miles south-east of Berlin. In 1900 his father was called to an important position in Berlin itself.
6. Paul Tillich, 'Autobiographical Reflections'; written for the volume *The Theology of Paul Tillich* ed. Charles W. Kegley and Robert W. Bretall, The Library of Living Theology, Macmillan, NY 1952, p. 8.
7. Paul Tillich, *The Protestant Era*, University of Chicago Press 1948, p. 163, and James Nisbet 1951.
8. *Ultimate Concern: Tillich in Dialogue* ed. D. Mackenzie Brown, Harper & Row and SCM Press 1965, p. 153.
9. Ibid., p. xv, from the biographical introduction by Cheever M. Brown.
10. Tillich, *The Interpretation of History*, pp. 15f.
11. Jaspers, 'Philosophical Autobiography', Schilpp, op. cit., p. 28.
12. Tillich, *The Interpretation of History*, p. 61.
13. Ibid., p. 35.
14. Tillich, *The Protestant Era*, p. 88. We might legitimately add: this is also dialectical thinking.
15. Jaspers, 'Reply to My Critics', written for Schilpp, op. cit., pp. 778f.
16. *Ultimate Concern*, p. 4.
17. Jaspers, 'Philosophical Autobiography', Schilpp, op. cit., p. 78.
18. Ibid.
19. Tillich, *The Interpretation of History*, p. 4.
20. *Ultimate Concern*, p. 181.
21. Tillich, 'Autobiographical Reflections', Kegley & Bretall, op. cit., p. 6.
22. Jaspers, 'Reply to My Critics', Schilpp, op. cit., p. 785.
23. Ibid., p. 784.
24. *Ultimate Concern*, p. 139.
25. Columbia University Press 1963. See especially pp. 81f.
26. *Ultimate Concern*, p. 76.
27. 'There is no blessedness where there is no conquest of the opposite possibility, and there is no life where there is no "otherness"', Paul Tillich, *Systematic Theology*, Vol 3, University of Chicago Press 1963 and James Nisbet 1964; reissued SCM Press 1978, p. 421.

Chapter 7 The Word and the Spirit

1. C. E. Raven, *Musings and Memories*, Martin Hopkinson 1931, p. 95.
2. In William Turner Levy and Victor Scherle, *Affectionately, T. S. Eliot: The Story of a Friendship 1947–1965*, Dent 1968, pp. 41f.

3. Tillich, *The Interpretation of History*, p. 7.

4. 'Ash Wednesday' I, in *Collected Poems 1909–1962*, p. 95.

5. Tillich, *The Interpretation of History*, p. 129.

6. Tillich, 'Reply to Interpretation and Criticism', written for Kegley & Bretall, op. cit., p. 346.

7. Eduard Heimann, 'Tillich's Doctrine of Religious Socialism', in Kegley & Bretall, op. cit., pp. 315f.

8. Tillich, *The Protestant Era*, p. xix.

9. Edwin Muir, 'The Killing' in *Collected Poems*, p. 225.

10. 'East Coker' IV, *Four Quartets*, in *Collected Poems 1909–1962*, p. 202.

11. Tillich, *Systematic Theology*, Vol 2, University of Chicago Press and James Nisbet 1957; reissued SCM Press 1978, p. 158.

12. Ibid., p. 159.

13. R. E. Pritchard, *D. H. Lawrence: Body of Darkness*, Hutchinson 1971, p. 207. Pritchard is quoting from the *Collected Letters* and from *Phoenix*.

14. 'An Ordinary Evening in New Haven', section ix, *The Collected Poems of Wallace Stevens*, pp. 471f.

15. Julian Huxley, *Religion without Revelation*, p. 379.

16. Karl Jaspers, *Tragedy is Not Enough*, Gollancz 1953, p. 16.

17. C. H. Dodd, *The Founder of Christianity*, p. 36.

18. 'The Dry Salvages' V, *Four Quartets*, in *Collected Poems 1909–1962*, pp. 212f.

19. Paul Tillich, *The Religious Situation*, Henry Holt & Co., NY 1932, p. 36.

20. Arnold Toynbee, *A Study of History*, one vol edn with additional material, OUP 1972, p. 486.

21. Ibid., p. 498.

22. *Phoenix II*, p. 438.

23. D. H. Lawrence, *Mornings in Mexico and Etruscan Places*, The Travel Books Vol III, Pheonix edn, Heinemann 1956, p. 49.

24. D. H. Lawrence, 'Poetry of the Present' (Introduction to the American edition of *New Poems 1918*), included in *The Complete Poems of D. H. Lawrence* ed. Vivian de Sola Pinta and Warren Roberts, Heinemann 1964, Vol 1, pp. 182ff.

25. Wallace Stevens, *Opus Posthumous*, Faber 1959, pp. 237f.

26. Ibid., pp. 236f.

27. Ibid., p. 238.

28. Quotations are from Jaspers' 'Philosophical Autobiography' and from his book *Man in the Modern Age*, Routledge 1933.

29. *Man in the Modern Age*, p. 203.

30. Karl Jaspers, *Way to Wisdom*, Gollancz and Yale University Press 1951, pp. 45f.

31. Edwin Muir, 'The Church', *Collected Poems*, pp. 262f.

32. D. H. Lawrence, *The Rainbow*, pp. 91f.